CIRCLE OF PARADOX:

TIME AND ESSENCE IN THE POETRY OF
JUAN RAMÓN JIMÉNEZ

CIRCLE OF PARADOX:

TIME AND ESSENCE IN THE POETRY OF JUAN RAMÓN JIMÉNEZ

PAUL R. OLSON

THE JOHNS HOPKINS PRESS, BALTIMORE, MARYLAND

To my wife

. . .*la primavera verdadera*. . .

PREFACE

It is surely no mere coincidence that the renewal of interest within this century in the philosophy of being has been accompanied by a similar renewal of interest in questions—nearly as old as those of 'first philosophy' itself—concerning the essence of poetry. To be sure, the origins of the two developments are quite distinct, and if Hugo Friedrich is right in tracing the rise of modern poetic theory to Rousseau and Diderot,[1] it even antedates that of the tradition of phenomenology and existentialism within which the new ontology has appeared. Yet it is clear that a certain convergence has occurred, if only as evidenced by the fact that a poet like Spain's Antonio Machado devoted so large a part of his later work to fundamental problems both of poetry and of existential ontology and that a professional philosopher like Heidegger, in whom the modern philosophy of being is fully established, has become interested in studying the essence of poetry in Hölderlin.

Even more important, however, may be the evidence offered in the thought and work of a writer like Juan Ramón Jiménez that the pursuit of pure poetry—poetry in its authentic being—leads itself to a consideration of the questions of first philosophy. So far as intellectual disciplines are concerned, Jiménez's area of activity was almost exclusively literary, and unlike Machado, he never undertook any systematic study of philosophy, al-

[1] See Hugo Friedrich, *La estructura de la lírica moderna*, trans. Juan Petit (Barcelona, 1959), pp. 27–34.

though it is known that he read Plato and probably some of the pre-Socratics. It was, however, exclusively as a poet that he regarded himself, and almost exclusively for and in poetry that he lived.

In his own country, the importance of that poetry was absolutely capital. Together with Antonio Machado, Jiménez initiated the modern Renaissance of the Spanish lyric which, virtually for the first time since the seventeenth century, has brought it international recognition. In addition, however, to the intrinsic literary qualities of his poetry (which in a body of work consisting of several thousand poems is naturally not always sustained on the highest level), there is, both for those who read it in the original and those who must rely on translations, a particular value in the study of Jiménez's work for what it reveals about the essence of all poetry, the relation of poetic essence to essence generally, and of both of them to time.

It must be emphasized that the study here presented is not one of time and essence with respect to the poetry of Jiménez but of that poetry itself, its forms of expression, and its principal themes, inductively identified as those of time and essence. This is, then, a work of explicative literary analysis, intended to arrive at as full an understanding as possible of the structure of meanings conveyed by the various levels of linguistic form which constitute the poetic *signifiant*. It is not, however, a comprehensive study of elements of style. Such a study is found in the work of Emmy Neddermann, which together with the addenda made to it in the review by Professor Raimundo Lida (see footnote references to both of these in Chapter II) can be considered nearly definitive. A more recent work of stylistic analysis, Sabine Ulibarri's *El mundo poético de Juan Ramón* (Madrid, 1962), has the advantage of including Jiménez's last work in its scope, but it was carried out without benefit of reference to Neddermann's complete study and does not surpass it in comprehensiveness.

Rather than attempting a general survey of the poet's expressive forms, these essays are based upon an interpretation of a limited number of them which recur throughout the whole body of work produced in more than half a century of creative activity, whose meanings, taken all together, constitute the central themes of the poetry as a whole. It is particularly fascinating to observe how the poetry of Juan Ramón's second period makes explicit many of the concepts which in the first period are present only as symbolic images and structures, the elucidation of which depends upon confrontation with the explicit expression of similar meanings in the later poetry, at the same time that the profundity of the latter is heightened by comparison with the earlier symbols.

Ancillary to this process of interpretation are certain references to analogous concepts in the work of various other poets and philosophers, which are adduced, not for the purpose of suggesting their direct influence in Jiménez or out of a gratuitous concern with parallels for their own sake, but for the purpose of providing additional means of access to the concepts themselves and, in some cases, of showing their archetypal—that is, universally human—character. Although the mode of exposition is occasionally deductive, the process of analysis was always inductive, the genesis of the entire book having occurred in the chance observation, some time ago, of the symmetrical structure of two of Jiménez's early poems. We always begin and end, then, with the poetry itself.

Earlier versions of Chapters II and III have appeared as separate articles, and an earlier version of Chapter IV was read as a paper in March, 1965, in the universities of Saint Andrews, Liverpool, and Bristol. All of them, however, have been subsequently revised and altered. Translations of verse and prose are entirely my own, as is the responsibility for any errors of interpretation which may occur in them. Verse is always quoted first in the original; prose is presented in translation only, except for a few passages from prose poems.

Permission to quote the poetry of Juan Ramón Jiménez has been granted on behalf of his heirs by Sr. Don Francisco Hernández-Pinzón Jiménez, to whom I express my sincerest thanks for this and innumerable other courtesies, particularly in allowing me to examine the unpublished manuscripts in his possession and in the Archivo Nacional de Historia of Madrid. For permission to translate poems covered by their English language rights in *Juan Ramón Jiménez: Three Hundred Poems, 1903–1953,* translated by Eloïse Roach, I thank the University of Texas Press. Other gratefully acknowledged debts of gratitude are those I owe to Professor Ricardo Gullón and Miss Raquel Sárraga, for much kind assistance during a period of work in the Sala Zenobia y Juan Ramón Jiménez in the Library of the University of Puerto Rico, and to the officers of the John Simon Guggenheim Memorial Foundation and the Spanish Fulbright Commission, with the aid of whose grants this book was written.

CONTENTS

CIRCLE OF PARADOX:

TIME AND ESSENCE IN THE POETRY OF JUAN RAMÓN JIMÉNEZ

The relation of time to the essential being of things has always been a basic problem of human existence and, in consequence, of the art and poetry of every age. But there is abundant reason to believe that artists of the past hundred years have both felt the problem more acutely, and at the same time achieved the conceptual insights necessary to understand it with greater clarity than ever before.

In an essay on the poetry of Jorge Guillén, Amado Alonso has observed that a particular mark of poets since Mallarmé has been the intensity of their concern to save what is lasting and essential from the certain wreckage of temporal existence,[1] and he adds that modern phenomenology has defined this concern and examined it in reference to all sciences of the mind, with the result that it can be seen as fundamental, not only in the creation of poetry, but in the genesis of language itself. For language is a logical act of exposition and differentiation by means of which the mind deliberately imposes upon the empirical truth of Heraclitus's *panta rhei* the Eleatic concept of static simultaneity, purely imaginary—that is, nonempirical—though it may be.[2]

---

[1] In *Materia y forma en poesía* (2a. ed.; Madrid, 1960), p. 294.
[2] This result is actually referred to in a work written in collaboration with Raimundo Lida, *El impresionismo en el lenguaje* (3a. ed.; Buenos Aires, 1956), pp. 187–88. I have in mind particularly an essay signed by both editors in which they comment with approval upon a passage in Ernst Cassirer's *Philosophie der symbolischen Formen* (Berlin, 1923) I, 247, in which language is regarded as a logical act of exposition and differentiation, through which "in dem stetigen Fluss des Bewusstseins erst irgendwelche

If, then, the concern of which Amado Alonso speaks is so profoundly rooted in the human mind as to constitute the origin of all human discourse, it must also be universally present, at some level of meaning, in that most consciously elaborated form of discourse which is poetry. It is clear, of course, that individual poets of every known epoch have felt this concern with varying degrees of clarity and insistence. It would obviously be vain to argue that any modern poet has surpassed Virgil, Petrarch, or Quevedo in his immediate personal awareness of the fugacity of life and human values, or that Horace, Garcilaso, or Ariosto were less aware than our contemporaries of the function of art in preserving essence. But what distinguishes the poetry of this past century, giving it a new common character, is, as Professor Alonso further points out, a necessity to differentiate that which 'exists' from that which 'is.'[3] Perhaps it might be added that in the past century, which has largely lost faith in other means of retaining values, the primary awareness discernible in older poets has been compounded by a new awareness, intuitive or consciously reasoned, of the significance for all poetry and for all activities of the mind of this imperative to preserve essences, and by a consequent new awareness of the poet's self as he responds to his own *Eheu, fugaces,* with an *Exegi monumentum.*

The problem of salvaging values from the flow of time has always presented poets with certain fundamental alternatives: on the one hand, that of dealing di-

---

Einschnitte entstehen, durch den das rastlose Kommen und Gehen der Sinneseindrücke gleichsam angehalten wird und gewisse Ruhepunkt gewinnt." The constant flow of consciousness is, of course, the subjective measure of the flow of time itself.
[3] *Materia y forma,* p. 294.

rectly with the objects and values with which the poet is concerned, presenting their 'being' within his poetry as effectively as he can; and, on the other hand, that of treating the phenomenon of time itself. Each of these in turn contains numerous other alternatives, but few, if any, are mutually exclusive; they will always allow for unique combinations, with varying degrees of emphasis upon some or others of them, and, of course, for unicity of expressive form. A third fundamental alternative, however, may be that of the balanced emphasis upon both time and the being of things which occurs when the explicit theme of a poem is the problem itself, that of salvaging something enduring from the wreckage of time. Spanish poetry of this century presents several notable examples of this type, as in Guillén's "Salvación de primavera" and Salinas's "Salvación por el cuerpo," and, as I hope to show, the whole of Juan Ramón Jiménez's poetic work may, indeed, be said to be devoted to the problem of this kind of 'salvation.' It should be clear, however, that in studying some aspects of time and essence ('being' made timeless) in the poetry of Juan Ramón, I do not look upon the themes themselves—themes of such absolute universality—as in any sense 'discoveries' within that poetry, but only as a fundamental ground upon which the poet's particularity is made manifest.

A large part of Jiménez's contribution to twentieth century poetry is in what he has shown us about the very nature of the poetic phenomenon, so that we have received from him as readers a fuller understanding of the whole of poetic literature, while poets coming after him have been enabled to perceive more clearly the basic goals of their art. Within the Hispanic world, this achievement is one which he shares with Antonio Machado, the poet who has most clearly formulated that necessity to distinguish 'existence' from 'being,' of which Amado Alonso has spoken.

In the case of Jiménez, these achievements in understanding are expressed partly through the example of his own life, dedicated wholly as it was to the poet's first duty, that of creation; partly through the testimony he gave of belief in the real existence of a *poesía pura*, understood, as he once put it, not as 'chemical poetry,' but simply as any *authentic* poetry.[4] Chiefly, however, it is in his poetry itself that these insights are to be found, and it will be a principal concern of this study, particularly in the following three chapters, to discuss certain aspects of the symbolic representation in that poetry of Juan Ramón's intuition of what all poetry attempts to do and be.

Machado's achievement, too, is probably pre-eminent within his poetry itself, but there is no doubt that the most explicit expression of his poetics occurs within the still poetic but fundamentally discursive philosophical prose to which his later years were dedicated. In any case, for several reasons Machado's poetic theories offer an excellent basis for insight into the theory and practice of Jiménez: in the first instance, because they are fully explicit; secondly, because their universal acceptance by succeeding generations of Spanish poets within this century gives them the character of a widely held conceptual system whose terminology is generally familiar; and finally, I believe, because of their intrinsic validity. To this it may be added that to approach the poetry of Jiménez from the poetics of Machado provides new insight into the differences and similarities be-

[4] "Poesía pura no es poesía casta, ni noble, ni química, ni aristocrática, ni abstracta. Es poesía auténtica, poesía de calidad." *El Sol* (February 23, 1936).

tween the two poets and may suggest the conclusion that their insights and sensibility are not so directly antithetical as is sometimes believed.

The portion of Machado's theories which chiefly concerns us here is his thought in regard to poetry and time, which is, to be sure, the very heart of his poetics. The apocryphal Juan de Mairena, whose "sentences, witticisms, notes, and memoires" express the philosophical and critical thought of Machado's years of maturity, has an *Arte poética,* which with ambiguous irony expresses that of Machado himself:

Juan de Mairena calls himself the *poet of time.* He used to assert that poetry was a temporal art—which many others had already said before him—and that the temporality proper to the lyric could be found fully expressed only in his verses. This somewhat naïve boast is that of a neophyte who comes to the world of letters prepared to write, not *for* everyone else, but *instead* of anyone else, and, in the final instance, *against* everyone else. In his *Arte poética* occur some violent paragraphs, in which Mairena presumes to assert the obtuseness of all who might maintain a thesis contrary to his own. We omit them as excessively vulgar, and go on to reproduce others, of more modesty and substance. "All arts," says Juan de Mairena in the first lesson of his *Arte poética,* "aspire to permanent creations, that is, to the fruits of intemporality. The so-called arts of time, such as music and poetry, are no exception. The poet pretends, in effect, that his work shall transcend the psychic moments in which it is produced. But we must not forget that it is, precisely, time (the vital time of the poet, with its own vibration) that the poet seeks to make timeless—or to put it more pompously—to make eternal. The poet that does not have a very marked temporal accent will be closer to logic than to the lyric."[5]

What Machado here calls the "vital time of the poet" is, of course, nothing other than the poet's very life, and

[5] Manuel y Antonio Machado, *Obras completas* (Madrid, 1957), p. 959.

7

the humor and irony with which this very serious statement is surrounded only enhance its profundity and give to it a reverberation which is that of Machado's own 'vital time.' In the best-known statement of his poetics, however, Machado spoke directly—without recourse, that is, to his alter ego—and even more explicity. This was in the *poética* written for the famous anthology of Gerardo Diego:

> In this year of your Anthology (1931) I think, as I did in the years of literary modernism (those of my youth), that poetry is the essential word in time. Modern poetry, which, as I understand it, begins, in part at least, with Edgar Poe, has been right up to the present day the history of the great problem presented to the poet by these two imperatives, which are in a certain sense contradictory: essentiality and temporality.[6]

The contrast between logic and poetry which appeared at the end of the statement of Juan de Mairena's poetics is presented in subsequent paragraphs in such a way as to show that it is precisely the temporal element which distinguished them. Logical thought, which masters ideas and captures essentials, is, according to Machado, a detemporalizing activity. The first principle of logic, which is that nothing exists which is not equal to itself, permits us "to anchor in the river of Heraclitus, yet not at all to imprison its fleeting wave."[7] For the poet, however, it is not possible to think outside of time, because what he thinks is his own life, which is, outside of time, absolutely nothing.

In the final portion of this *poética,* Machado expressed his disagreement with poets of the generation current at the time, chiefly because of their tendency to

---

[6] Gerardo Diego, *Poesía española contemporánea* (Madrid, 1962), p. 149. This volume is a reprinting of the editions of 1932 and 1934.
[7] *Ibid.*

detemporalize and intellectualize poetry. He denied the possibility of a lyric of the intellect but ultimately granted that the intellect can at least serve poetry by satisfying the imperative to essentiality, which he had already asserted to be a co-ordinate and complement to temporality within the poetic phenomenon, although the two are "in some sense contradictory."

It is, in any case, this intuition of the two imperatives and the paradox of their polar complementary which is particularly significant with respect to the poetry of Jiménez, in which their contradictory character is felt, not merely "in a certain sense," but completely. This phenomenon is, indeed, part of a general one in his poetry, in which affective intensity is often achieved through the tension of paradox, of contradiction, or a sense of simultaneous being and non-being. Although he never referred to the contradiction as explicitly as does Machado, and although his poetic theory and concepts of human life are even less systematic than Machado's, it can, I believe, be shown that his intuition into these fundamentals of poetry is basically in accord with that of his great contemporary.

One of the primary characteristics of the poetry of Juan Ramón is, indeed, its temporality, by which it expresses, with striking profundity of intuition, the perpetual mutability and elusiveness of all beloved objects. This quality is a constant in the whole of his work, but perhaps it is most immediately striking in his First Period, previous to the *Diario de un poeta recién casado* (1917),[8]—the period in which he was most under the

[8] The two principal periods in the poetic trajectory of Juan Ramón Jiménez to which I refer here and elsewhere can, of course, be divided further, but most critics would probably grant the basic validity of this broad twofold division. Gonzalo Sobejano

influence of Verlainean symbolism and the Spanish romantic, Bécquer, for whom the essence of poetry is
expressed in the luminous wake of a shooting star and
in countless other images of fugacity.[9] At one point,
when this manner was at the height of its development
in Jiménez's work, he described the temporality of poetry
within the prologue to the third section of *La soledad
sonora* (1911) with a statement which was, at the time,
his definition of poetry itself:

Poetry, like a landscape, like lyrical water, is nothing precise, nor defined, nor immutable. Like its sister, music, it
has emotion as its rose and wandering as its star.

Like an evening sky, in which spiritual colors bear the
soul from fantasy to fantasy, poetry must be errant and in-
decisive, a wellspring of vague beauty, a breeze of sensations.

Infinite vagueness of forms and tones, in which ideal
gardens of roses, flesh, souls, or clouds flourish in inex-
tinguished succession; light of countless nuances, apparition
brought by every melody of unknown origin, borne by every
wind of the eternal, poetry, a woman of mist, is the indelible
essence of life.[10]

---

infers such a consensus from the summary of trajectory studies
included in his "Juan Ramón Jiménez a través de la crítica,"
Romanistisches Jahrbuch, VIII (1957), 341–66, and it can be
confirmed in such standard works as those of Emmy Neddermann
(see note 11), Enrique Díez-Canedo, *Juan Ramón Jiménez en su
obra* (México, 1944), and Graciela Palau de Nemes, *Vida y obra
de Juan Ramón Jiménez* (Madrid, 1957). More recent studies by
Guillermo Díaz-Plaja, *Juan Ramón Jiménez en su poesía* (Madrid, 1958) and Bernardo Gicovate, *La poesía de Juan Ramón
Jiménez* (San Juan, Puerto Rico; 1959) distinguish many more
periods, but all of them could probably be assigned to one or the
other of the two primary categories. Antonio Sánchez-Barbudo
subscribes to the majority opinion in *La segunda época de Juan
Ramón Jiménez* (Madrid, 1962). There is, then, a general agree-
ment that the *Diario* represents the most basic turning point in
the poet's career.

[9] *Rimas,* V and III.

[10] *Primeros libros de poesía* (Madrid, 1959), p. 999. Quotations
from this volume will hereafter be designated in parentheses by
the abbreviation *PLP* followed by the page number and, if not
already identified in the context, by a brief form of the title of

Change, movement, and the lack of fixed forms—all
are the measure of temporality, and in Jiménez's early
poetry the qualities of mutability, errancy, and tran-
sience are suggested in countless details: scenes set in
the transitional seasons of spring and fall or at the
transitional hours of dawn and dusk; an abundance of
delicate, 'transitional' colors—mauve, rose, *mate,* or
unique shades like "a non-color, almost green."[11] Temporality is suggested too by the constant flow of water in
fountains and arroyos, by the music which wanders
through the night, and be the fact that objects are so
frequently seen in the perspective of flight, so that their
only visible facet is the obverse.[12] In all of these details,
and many more, the poetry of Jiménez displays the
marked temporal accent which Machado regarded as
definitive in distinguishing all true poetry from rhymed
logic.

In addition, however, to the quality of temporality,
and often concomitant with it, this poetry also contains
with great frequency a note of quietude, of contemplative ecstasy expressive of the longing for the eternal
which may be equated with Machado's 'imperative to

---

the original book. Quotations from *Libros de poesía* (Madrid,
1959) are identified in a similar way, using the abbreviation *LP;*
those from the *Segunda antolojía* (2a. ed.; Madrid, 1959), first
published in 1922, by *SA;* those from the *Tercera antolojía*
(Madrid, 1957) by *TA*. In order that the chronological aspect of
the quotations be kept clear, reference should be made to the
Appendix.

[11] *LP* 131, *Estío.* The use of color in the poetry of Jiménez has been
studied in detail in Emmy Neddermann, *Die symbolistischen
Stilelemente im Werke von Juan Ramón Jiménez* (Hamburg,
1935), pp. 80–102, and in Paul Verdevoye, "Coloripoesía de Juan
Ramón Jiménez," *La Torre,* V (1957), 245–82.

[12] See Fernand Verhesen, "Tiempo y espacio en la obra de Juan
Ramón Jiménez," *La Torre,* V (1957), 97. See also Ricardo
Gullón, *Estudios sobre Juan Ramón Jiménez* (Buenos Aires,
1960), pp. 152–60.

essentiality.' At times it takes the form of a direct expression of the desire for eternity, as in these lines from *La soledad sonora:*

> ¡Cielo, pájaro, sol! ¡No quiero, mientras viva,
> más que esta tarde azul, de armonía y de oro!
> ¡Ah, quién pudiera prolongar eternamente
> este instante de música, de fragancia y de canto!
> *(PLP* 914)

> *Sky, bird, and sun! While I live, I wish*
> *no more than this blue afternoon, of harmony and gold!*
> *Oh, if I could prolong eternally*
> *this instant of music, of fragrance and song!*

In such a moment, of course, the poet expresses not only his desire to halt the flow of time but also the poignant recognition of the impossibility of the desire. There are moments, however, when the contemplative quietude is so profound that time seems actually to have stopped. As, for example, in the early *Jardines lejanos:*

> Los árboles no se mueven;
> todo está en éxtasis; quietos
> están los dulces cristales
> de las fuentes, los senderos
> parece que no se van;
> las flores miran al cielo,
> y los árboles contemplan
> sus sombras fijas. . . , *(PLP* 422)

> *The trees are motionless;*
> *Everything is in ecstasy, and quiet*
> *stand the fair crystals*
> *of the fountains; even the paths*
> *   seem to go nowhere;*
> *the flowers gaze at the sky,*
> *the trees behold*
> *their motionless shadows. . .*

The study of Emmy Neddermann has shown how this static quality, too, is expressed in numerous details of form, and she has consequently been led to see in the poet himself "weniger ein dynamisches als statisches Weltgefühl,"[13] but clearly the static aspects of Juan Ramón's poetry must be understood in terms which take account of the kinetic aspects as well. As a profoundly contemplative and lyrical poet, Jiménez doubtless tends very strongly to evoke the mood of ecstasy, and the movement of narrative or discursive language is almost wholly absent from his poetry. Within his apparently static images, however, there can be felt the vital palpitation which is nothing other than the rhythmic flow of time itself.

Certainly the antivital implications of a pure stasis were evident to Juan Ramón, and he constantly sought to retain within the static moment the kinetic qualities of life itself. The ideal, as he expressed it in an aphorism of his *Ética estética,* was "An ecstasy which does not kill what is alive."[14] Anxious longing and pursuit and even falling back in failure are aspects of human experience which can be preserved in their authentic reality only if their intrinsic temporality is preserved as well, and although in Jiménez's later years the moments when his poetry expresses the joy of possession become increasingly frequent, the long period which preceded these moments produced a poetry expressive chiefly of the pursuit of objects of beauty which are themselves in constant flight through time. The dynamics of desire within the poet and of elusiveness within its objects are, like the dynamics of life itself, essential to each of them,

[13] *Die symbolistischen Stilelemente,* p. 4.
[14] Francisco Garfias (ed.), *Cuadernos de Juan Ramón Jiménez* (Madrid, 1960), p. 200.

and Jiménez strives to preserve these dynamics in an eternal—but not purely static—perception of the essences which transcend and survive temporal existence.

For Machado, the concept of essence was doubtless quite specifically Husserlian, even though he may have had no direct knowledge of the phenomenologists of Freiburg until shortly before the Spanish civil war.[15] It is, nevertheless, quite true that the concept of 'that which is' in modern poetry is generally closer to the 'essence' of phenomenology than to the 'ideas' of Platonism, as Amado Alonso suggests in the essay quoted at the beginning of this chapter,[16] and it is fairly likely that Machado's use of the term ought to be so described. The fact that his principal interest was in temporality means, however, that the precise nature of the concept of essence is of secondary importance, and it must be granted that he refers to it usually only in contrast to the imperative to temporality.

In the thought of Jiménez, it is certainly not possible to find any technical definition of essence, but it seems not unlikely that he, in contrast, would have accepted a definition of 'that which is' in terms of the Platonic tradition. "I am, was, and will be a Platonist," he wrote

---

[15] Julian Marías has pointed out in "Machado y Heidegger," *Insula*, No. 94 (1953), that Machado's acquaintance with *Sein und Zeit* is almost certainly indirect, and he has convincingly identified the source of some of his discussions of Heidegger as a brief work by Georges Gurvitch, *Les tendences actuelles de la philosophie allemande* (Paris, 1930), a Spanish translation of which appeared in 1931. The same volume contained also an exposition of the thought of Husserl, whom Machado had not read as late as in 1926, according to A. Sánchez Barbudo, *Estudios sobre Unamuno y Machado* (Madrid, 1959), p. 229, and he may not, therefore, have known his work before reading Gurvitch.
[16] *Materia y forma*, p. 294.

to Luis Cernuda in 1943,[17] and more than once he asserts his acceptance of Plato's definition of poetry itself. For the review *Caracola* he wrote in 1954:

Until an unsuspected miracle appears to tell us something better, I accept the ancient definition of Plato. Yes, for me poetry is something divine, winged, full of grace, expression of the charm and mystery of the world. (Divine here means original, primal, since God in his name is nothing but beginning and origin.) "[18]

Probably even more important than such testimony is the expression within his poetry itself of Platonic concepts of universals, but more must be said of this in Chapter III.

For the moment it is enough to point out that his concept of essence must usually be understood as subsumed in that of eternity, that obverse of the concept of time which is the realm in which essences are to be found. Certainly, in any case, the terms 'eternity' and 'eternal' are much more frequent in both his verse and his prose than 'essence.' As for the particular concept of eternity which Jiménez held, what has already been said about his rejection of absolute quietude should make it clear that he did not regard eternity merely as 'stopped time,' for he realized that mortality and temporal brevity are themselves a part of all beloved entities, and if their total reality is to have any eternity at all, it must be one of depth, immanent within time itself. In the studies which follow it will, I believe, become clear that for Jiménez eternity and the essences within it are the permanent realities which survive the

---

[17] The letter has been reprinted in Juan Ramón Jiménez, *La corriente infinita* (Madrid, 1961); the passage quoted is from p. 178.
[18] *La corriente infinita*, p. 218.

passing of every moment, every being, every *thing*, and which forever *are* because they once have been.

Man, of course, can perceive these realities only in memory, and for that very reason Jiménez could at one moment express his eagerness for the present moment to pass in order that its essence might become the possession of memory. Thus, in *Piedra y cielo,* he writes:

> Este istante
> que ya va a ser recuerdo, ¿qué es?
> Música loca,
> que trae estos colores que no fueron
> —pues que fueron
> de aquella tarde de oro, amor y gloria;
> esta música
> que va a no ser, ¿qué es?
> ¡Istante, sigue, sé recuerdo
> —recuerdo, tú eres más, porque tú pasas,
> sin fin, la muerte con tu flecha—,
> sé recuerdo, conmigo ya lejano!
> . . . ¡Oh, sí, pasar, pasar, no ser istante,
> sino perenidad en el recuerdo!
> ¡Memoria inmensa mía,
> de istantes que pasaron hace siglos;
> eternidad del alma de la muerte!
> . . . ¡Istante, pasa, pasa tú que eres—¡ay!—
> yo!
>
> Este istante, este tú,
> que va ya a ser muriendo, ¿qué es?
>   *(LP* 702–03)

> *This moment*
> *which is already becoming memory, what is it?*
> *Mad music,*
> *which brings these colors that were not*
> *—because they were*
> *of that evening of gold, of love, and glory;*
> *this music*
> *which is about to not be, what is it?*
> *Moment, move on, be memory*

> *—memory, you are greater, for you pass*
> *through death eternally, with your arrow—,*
> *be memory, when I am far away!*
> *. . . Oh, yes, pass on, pass on, to be not a moment,*
> *but permanence in memory!*
> *   Vast memory of mine,*
> *of moments passed centuries since;*
> *eternity of the soul of death!*
> *. . . Moment, pass on, pass on, you who are—alas!—*
> *myself!*
>
> *This moment, this you,*
> *which is about to be by dying, what is it?*

Of principal interest to us at this point is the fact that the poem expresses the intuition that produced a complete reversal in the poet's attitude toward the past. Beginning with the assumption that the passing of the present and its experience into the past constitutes a transition from being into non-being, he suddenly sees that remembered experience is greater than present experience, for it is as memory that an experience triumphs over the passing of time and becomes eternal. Indeed, as Jiménez concludes in the final lines, it is only by 'dying' (that is, moving into the past), that the experience of the present moment and the self which is the subject of that experience really begin to 'be,' to 'have essence.' In so far as the intuition contains—or rather, constitutes—a definition of essence, it is, in fact, identical with that of Hegel and Sartre, for whom essence is 'what has been,'[19] although Jiménez's idealism

---

[19] Jean-Paul Sartre, *Being and Nothingness*, trans. Hazel E. Barnes (New York, 1956), p. 120. In the opening pages of the same work Sartre gives a definition of essence which emphasizes, not its grounding in the past, but rather its character as the sum of all the appearances of an existent: "The essence of an existent is no longer a property sunk in the cavity of this existent; it is

leads him to regard it still as an inner and higher reality for which the existent entity is but an outer shell. It will be important, then, to keep this poem in mind when considering the 'Platonism' of Jiménez in Chapter III, since it clearly states his concept of the objective reality of 'ideas,' essences, and universals.

The concept is, in fact, one which permits him to be both a 'realist' and a 'nominalist,' for through it he could have accepted fully the nominalist dictum, *universalia sunt nomina,* and then added, *nomina sunt realia.* In a brief but striking poem on the very purpose of poetic art (which he wrote to a poet friend in 1911), he says:

> Del amor y las rosas,
> no ha de quedar sino los nombres.
> ¡Creemos los nombres! (*TA* 254)[20]

---

the manifest law which presides over the succession of its appearances, it is the principle of the series. . . Essence, as the principle of the series, is definitely only the concatenation of appearances; that is, itself an appearance." (See p. xlvi of *Being and Nothingness.*) More similar than either of these definitions to the sentiment in Jiménez's poem is Sartre's analysis of the poet's feeling for the past in his *Baudelaire* (Paris, 1947), p. 196 ff.

[20] The whole of this poem will be quoted and commented upon in chap. IV, but it is well to note here a possible source for this concept in Unamuno's early novel, *Amor y pedagogía* (1902), in which don Fulgencio Entrambosmares, in whom rationalistic philosophy is caricaturized, tells his pupil Apolodoro: "Cuando se hayan reducido por completo las cosas a ideas desaparecerán las cosas quedando las ideas tan sólo, y reducidas estas últimas a nombres quedarán sólo los nombres y el eterno e infinito silencio pronunciándolos en la infinidad y por toda una eternidad." There can, of course, be little doubt that Jiménez read the novel, and if when he wrote the poem, the concept was no longer a conscious memory, it is, nevertheless, clear that it would appeal to any poet of the symbolist tradition. A further echo of it can, in fact, be found in the *Cántico* of Jorge Guillén: "¿Y las rosas? Pestañas/ Cerradas: horizonte/ Final. ¿Acaso nada?/ Pero quedan los nombres."

Of love and roses,
Nothing will remain but the names.
Let us create names!

The world of created names, which is the world of
poetry, survives the passing of love and life and beauty
because, in the first instance, the entities of which it is
constituted have at least the possibility of preservation
in their empirical existence beyond the lives of their
creators. But, in a profounder sense, that world is eternal because behind the empirical form of every word,
every 'name,' stands the phenomenon of meaning,
which is the essence of the objects to which it refers and
is timeless—in effect, eternal—because experience reveals that it can and does survive the passing of both its
signifiants and its referends.[21]

The idea that linguistic meaning, the psychic content
of any verbal artifact, is eternal and independent of the
fate of the artifact as an empirical entity is fully developed in the first poem in *Belleza*, in which the 'verbal
artifact' is actually the whole of Jiménez's poetic work:

> Sé que mi Obra es lo mismo
> que una pintura en el aire;
> que el vendaval de los tiempos
> la borrará toda, como
> si fuese perfume o música;
> que quedará sólo de ella
> —sí arruinado en nóes—
> al gran silencio solar,
> la ignorancia de la luna.
> —No, no; ella, un día, será
> (borrada) esistencia inmensa,

[21] It has seemed useful to employ the terminology of Ferdinand de
Saussure in his analysis of the linguistic sign. See his *Cours de
linguistique générale* (Paris, 1922), pp. 99 and 144.

desveladora virtud,
será, como el antesol,
imposible norma bella;
sinfín de angustioso afán,
mina de excelso secreto. . .
¡Mortal flor mía inmortal
reina del aire de hoy! (*LP* 985)

    I know that my Work is like
a painting in the air;
that the winds of time
will cancel it all, as if
it were perfume or music;
that of it will remain only
—a ruined yes among the no's—
in the great solar silence,
the ignorance of the moon.
    No, no; it will one day be
(when canceled) an immense existence,
a power-giver of consciousness;
it will be, like the first sun,
impossible norm of beauty;
eternity of anxious longing,
a mine of lofty secret . . .
Immortal and mortal flower, mine,
ruler of this day's realm of air!

The world of words may, then, disappear as an empirical entity, but the essences which are its meanings are eternal. When Jiménez writes that only names will remain, he clearly is looking beyond their empirical entities to those essences. This, indeed, was his constant tendency in all his efforts at *depuración* and the improvement of poems through revision (reliving, he called it) of form so as to make it as transparent as possible and ultimately to disappear. In the notes to the *Segunda antolojía poética,* he declares:

Perfection—simplicity, spontaneity—of form is not vulgar neglect of form nor the virtuosity of a self-conscious Baroque

20

architect; for in both cases one becomes entangled in the form itself; it calls our attention constantly, making us stumble; rather it is that absolute precision which makes form disappear, leaving only the content to exist, to "be" itself the content. (*SA* 324)

It has been claimed that in these lines Jiménez revives the no longer tenable Aristotelian distinction between 'form' and 'content,'[22] but it seems clear that his ideal, actually, is to de-emphasize the distinction by making external form as unobtrusive as possible, and the last words imply a complete synthesis of the two through the subsuming of form into content. The intention, clearly, is to strive toward an autonomy of the *signifié*—that is, linguistic content—and although the achievement of that goal may be recognized as impossible, the purpose of the effort, clearly, is to be able to regard the essence represented by the *signifié* as salvable from temporal wreckage, from the passing of all empirical forms, both verbal and material.[23] The material forms are, of course, the objects whose names the poet seeks to create—objects whose disappearance is as inevitable as that of the verbal forms themselves—but between name and object stands the phenomenon of meaning, which the poet's idealism sees as the primary and virtually autonomous entity.

It is generally recognized that in most uses of language, meaning is a combination of objective denotation and affective and allusive connotation; that it requires, in fact, a very particular effort for humans to eliminate all but the denotative meanings from their

[22] See Jean-Louis Schonberg, *Juan Ramón Jiménez ou le chant d'Orphée* (Neuchâtel, 1961), p. 138.
[23] A similar linguistic interpretation has been given to Jorge Guillén's use of *alma* (soul), in Joaquín González Muela, *La realidad y Jorge Guillén* (Madrid, 1962), p. 54.

speech; and that such an effort is probably fully successful only through the creation of new symbolic systems such as those of mathematics. For the poet, however, as Dámaso Alonso has emphasized, linguistic meaning is extremely complex, not only in its richness of connotation but in its denotative precision as well.[24] For Jiménez, it is because objects and their names are regarded with love that they contain an infinite depth of meaning, and it is this infinity which gives them the quality of eternity.

Such an eternity may at times be perceived within the very briefest of temporal limits, and Jiménez gives frequent expression to his awareness of this truth. In the *Diario de un poeta recién casado,* for example, a charming poem describes the moment in which a young mother lifts up her child to reach for the cherries of a tree in a rose garden. It ends with the exclamation:

> ¡Amor y vida
> se funden, como el cielo con la tierra,
> en un esplendor suave
> que es, un istante, eterno! (*LP* 358)

> *Love and life*
> *are fused, like heaven with the earth,*
> *in a gentle splendor,*
> *which is, for one instant, eternal!*

It is love which reveals the depth of meaning and of meaningfulness in the brief moment, thereby revealing too the eternity which is uniquely its own. To call a thing eternal-for-an-instant, however, is to speak in a paradox, and we thus have here an example of one type

---

[24] Dámaso Alonso, *Poesía española,* (3a. ed.; Madrid, 1957), pp. 19–33.

of paradox which has been mentioned previously as constituting a principal source of affective and logical tension within this poetry. The only possible conceptual resolution of the paradox is to see the eternity of the instant as an infinity of depth, a dimension which intersects the linear successiveness of time at every moment. This depth is, then, the *qualitas* of the moment, that is, its essence, and therefore the paradox of the eternal instant is clearly a reflex of the primary pradox of temporality and essentiality.

Another frequent paradox in Jiménez is that of the synthesis of a concept of motion with one of quietude or rest. In the early Juan Ramón, whose verses are so markedly colored by the Verlainean tone, the principal image of this paradox is the fountain (which will be studied in detail in Chapter II). It may be exemplified here with some lines from the book which marks Jiménez's entrance into the first period of plenitude, the *Arias tristes:*

> Pastor, toca un aire dulce
> y quejumbroso en tu flauta,
> llora en estos valles llenos
> de languidez y añoranza;
> llora la hierba del suelo,
> llora el diamante del agua,
> llora el ensueño del sol
> y los ocasos del alma. (*PLP* 304–305)

> *Shepherd, play a melody,*
> *sweet and plaintive, on your flute;*
> *weep within these valleys, filled*
> *with languor and melancholy;*
> *weep the grasses of the ground,*
> *weep the diamond of water,*
> *weep the daydream of the sun*
> *and the sunsets of the soul.*

23

The diamond of water, combining a gemlike permanence with eternal motion, is, then, a perfect icon of the synthesis of contemplative stasis and vital kinesis, that is, of essentiality and temporality.

In his later years, Jiménez gave this phenomenon the name *éstasis dinámico,* and he used it on more than one occasion to express his concepts of art and poetry. In "Poesía y literatura," a lecture delivered at the University of Miami in 1939, he says that "the poetic state of grace, dynamic ecstasy, . . . is the form of flight, the impassioned form of liberty."[25] But if dynamic ecstasy is the 'state of grace' antecedent to poetic creation, it is also present in the completed work. The concept (though not the term itself) is strikingly expressed in a brief poem from *Poesía:*

> ¡Hervor costante y sin fin,
> de mi trabajo; inquietud
> y contención, en un cáliz!
> —En un punto, chispa inmensa
> y breve, de puntas libres
> y de redondez esclava.—
> ¡Ola ardiente; sentimiento
> y fuego, bajo la copa
> de la voluntad alegre! (*LP* 968)

> *Constant and endless seething*
> *of my work; disquiet*
> *and contention, in a chalice!*
> *—Within a single point, a spark immense*
> *and brief, with free rays*
> *and with subjected roundness.—*
> *An ardent wave, a sentiment*
> *and fire, beneath the cup*
> *of the joyous will!*

[25] The lecture is reprinted in *El trabajo gustoso* (México, 1961), which will subsequently be referred to by the abbreviation *TG.* (This quotation is from p. 40.)

Ultimately, however, Juan Ramón will see that dynamic ecstasy is fundamental in art because it is the very condition of life itself. In the lecture entitled "La razón heroica," delivered in Buenos Aires in 1948 as part of a cycle on poetry and life, he says:

> Yes, I insist; one must consider life as dynamic ecstasy, as action in thought or in sentiment, and not as static dynamism, because this would only be detained spiritual movement. Dynamic ecstasy is absolute romanticism, absolute heroism.[26]

The contrast established here between "action in thought" and "detained spiritual movement" is significant also with respect to what has previously been said concerning Juan Ramón's awareness of the antivital implications of *stasis* as such, and it represents a further important modification of what earlier criticism has had to say about the poet's static *Weltgefühl*.

Concepts of dynamism and motion suggest, in the first instance, movement in space, but obviously temporal motion is always implicit in them. In the poetry of Juan Ramón, the latter concept is actually the primary one. If for Aristotle time is the 'number of movement,' for Jiménez motion is, above all, the measure of time, and therefore this second paradox is also a clear analogue of the basic one of essentiality and temporality. 'Dynamic ecstasy' is, then, simply Juan Ramón's way of saying both 'time within essence' and 'essence within time,' and in so far as it is a principle of poetic art, it is strikingly similar to Machado's definition of poetry as "the essential word in time."

A third type of paradox is that found in the deliberate juxtaposition of concepts of magnitude and brevity,

[26] *TG*, p. 136.

as in the image of the "spark immense and brief" in the
poem last quoted, or in these lines from *Belleza:*

> ¡Obra, ola leve e infinita,
> conciencia dividida—y una—
> de todos los momentos de mi ser!
> ¡Firme delicadeza
> de istantes permanentes,
> que habrás de resistir con tu cristal humano
> —partido e integral como el diamante—,
> el traqueteo y el silbido,
> la vociferación y el golpetazo,
> el eco y el empuje
> del mundo éste de los feos hombres!
> Nada derrumbará ni aplastará
> tus jigantescas rosas diminutas,
> pájaro prodijioso;
> corazonazo continente
> de corazones incontables
> —uno por cada hecho de mi vida—;
> nada te quebrará las suaves alas
> con las que subes, recta y rápida, al cenit,
> ingrávida en tu inmensa pesantez,
> más grande en cada ojo, en cada grito tuyo
> que todo el universo! (*LP* 1057–58)

> *Poetic work, a wave both light and infinite,*
> *consciousness divided—and yet one—*
> *of all the moments of my being!*
> *Firm delicacy*
> *of permanent moments,*
> *who must resist with your human crystal*
> *—parted yet integral, like the diamond—,*
> *the clatter and the shrillness,*
> *the shouting and the blows,*
> *the echo and the shoving*
> *of this world of ugly men!*
> *Nothing will throw down or crush*
> *your roses, gigantic and diminutive,*
> *prodigious wing;*
> *heartbeat containing*
> **uncountable hearts**

26

—one for each moment of my life—;
nothing will break the smooth wings
with which you ascend, straight and swift, to the zenith,
ingravid in your immense heaviness,
greater in each eye, in each of your cries,
than the whole universe!

It has been necessary to quote the entire poem, for paradox abounds in it, from the "consciousness divided—and yet one" to the final concept of the work as greater in each eye than the whole universe. In the final lines, and in the image of the "roses, gigantic and diminutive," are the examples of the paradox of magnitude in brevity, which most concern us here.

All of these paradoxes quite naturally bring to mind the language of the mystics, and in later chapters there will occur frequent references to parallels between the language of Jiménez and the mystic mode of expression. With respect to the paradox here discussed, however, it seems appropriate to point out its similarity to a maxim of Master Eckhart: *In Divinis, quodlibet est in quolibet et maximum in minimo.* 'In things Divine, all is in all and the greatest in the least,' a formula which became the very basis of the philosophy of Nicholas of Cusa and had an immense influence on Leonardo da Vinci and Giordano Bruno.[27] Perhaps the clearest expression of the paradox of magnitude in brevity in the work of Jiménez is in the prose poem, *Espacio:*

Great is brevity, and if we wish to be and seem greater, let us gather only with love, not quantity. The sea is nothing more than gathered drops; love nothing more than gathered murmurings; and you, cosmos, nothing more than little

[27] Heinrich Denifle, "Meister Eckeharts lateinische Schriften," *Archiv für Litteratur-und-Kirchengeschichte des Mittelalters,* II (1886), 571. Cited in Georges Poulet, *Les métamorphoses du cercle* (Paris, 1961), p. xii.

worlds united. The most beautiful thing is the ultimate atom, the sole indivisible one, which for being so is no longer small. (*TAP* 856)

In most of the poetry of the first decade of his Second Period, Jiménez took this paradox as a creative principle, and constantly sought to express a maximum of poetic sentiment with a minimum of words. The letter to Luis Cernuda quoted earlier contains in another context an apology of this creative practice, in the rationale of which this same paradox plays a crucial part:

The important thing in poetry, for me, is the quality of eternity which a poem may leave in one who reads it with no idea of time, concentrated quality which will be to him who tastes it like an unending ideal diamond, tiny, with an immense aura. The poem is seed more than fruit, secret soul of any life. Love, which is the supreme poetry and science of human life—I don't know if you are aware of this—is inevitably brief; the rose and the prayer are also on only points of tangency for totality. An immanent poetry is itself and everything. Immanence without size. What is size?[28]

If, in any poem, the 'quality of eternity' is the important thing, and quantity or size is negligible, it is clear that the key to the resolution of this paradox is in the qualitative meaning of concepts of immensity for Juan Ramón. This is true, for example, in the famous dedicatory phrase, "A la inmensa minoría," which he used from 1923 on, although, by a curious additional paradox, the metaphoric and literal values in adjective and noun might also be reversed. Thus, in an explanation of the phrase written after he came to America, Jiménez says:

If anyone in the uncultured majority comes to understand poetry to a sufficient degree, he no longer is of the majority; for some reason, no matter what, he is of the minority. When

[28] *La corriente infinita*, p. 178.

I accepted from Antonio Marichalar the motto, "To the immense minority," it was after having understood it finally in this sense, and in this way I continue to understand and write it.[29]

He then adds that it is perfectly possible for the whole of society to become 'minority' in this sense, thus making the noun the metaphoric and qualitative term, and allowing the adjective its literal quantitative meaning:"And I shall always think of an immense minority, which might one day come to be total, and like an aristocracy, in relation to the democracy which is provisional and subjective." This latter thought may well have been a new development in Juan Ramón's understanding of the motto, motivated by a desire to mitigate and perhaps explain away its tone of aristocratic hauteur, at a time when the liberal democracy which he always supported intellectually was under attack from an alliance of reactionary forces. There is no reason to believe that he would earlier have rejected such a corollary, but it has the quality of a rationalization—a very admirable one—of an aristocratic instinct which might well have led to political sympathies of quite a different sort. It is understandable, therefore, that Jiménez's phrase has become the object of polemical attack from the democratically inclined poets of Spain's postwar era, inspiring in one of them the opposing motto, "A la inmensa mayoría."[30]

Despite the reversal given to the literal and metaphoric—that is, the qualitative and quantitative—elements in the phrase by his later interpretation of it, Juan Ramón's motto still exemplifies the paradox of

[29] *La corriente infinita,* p. 290.
[30] Blas de Otero uses this phrase as the title for a poem in *Pido la paz y la palabra* (Santander, 1955).

'the greatest in the least,' both in terms of the earlier explanation itself and because the later one can, I think, be understood only within the awareness of the paradox as its starting point.

The principle of 'the greatest in the least' may not, at first, seem directly analogous to the paradoxical synthesis of temporality and essentiality, and it is, indeed, at some remove from it; but clearly the immensity which is qualitative is of the realm of essence, and literal quantitative dimensions are of the empirical world of space and time. Thus our third paradox, too, may be seen as analogous to and ultimately derived from that of the tension between time and essence.

A fourth type of paradox is one borrowed directly from St. John of the Cross in the phrase *la soledad sonora*, 'the sounding solitude.'[31] It appears, in fact, as the title of a book by Jiménez published in 1911, but the phrase itself, or a variant of it, appears elsewhere with sufficient frequency to constitute an identifiable type. Thus, in the *Poemas mágicos y dolientes:*

> Nadie. . . , ni voz, ni voto. . . La soledad sonora,
> plena de ritmos de oro y de muda elocuencia;
> escuchar lo ignorado, lo nuevo, hora tras hora,
> en una dulce y perfumada negligencia. . . (*PLP* 1083)

> *No one. . . , neither voice nor prayer. . . The sound-*
> *ing solitude,*
> *full of golden rhythms and of mute eloquence;*
> *hearing what is unknown and new, hour after hour,*
> *within a sweet and perfumed negligence. . .* [32]

[31] "Canciones entre el alma y el esposo," stanza 15:
    "la noche sosegada
    en par de los levantes del aurora,
    la música callada,
    la soledad sonora,
    la cena que recrea y enamora."

[32] See also *PLP* 796.

The 'mute eloquence' in the second of these lines is, of
course, the direct complement of the 'sounding solitude,' just as in John of the Cross its complement had
been *música callada,* 'silent music.' Both complementary
phrases make it clear that *la soledad sonora* means not
only 'sounding solitude' but 'sounding silence' as well,
and it is, therefore—in both poets—a bold and direct
paradox.

Variants of the same concept are also numerous. One
of the most frequently anthologized poems in the book
whose title quotes St. John begins,

> Un pájaro, en la lírica calma del mediodía,
> canta bajo los mármoles del palacio sonoro; *(PLP* 936)

> *A bird, within the lyric calm of noon,*
> *sings beneath the marbles of the sonorous palace. . .*

and expresses the concept both in 'lyric calm' and in
'sonorous palace.' Several years later, in *Belleza,* the
play of similar paradoxes becomes really quite complex
in a brief poem about music, in which heard sounds are
likened to an

> Oscuridad luciente, como
> un diamante en la noche;
> como un prismático llorar no oído; *(LP* 1016)

> *Bright darkness, like*
> *a diamond in the night;*
> *like a prismatic weeping never heard;*

The music, therefore, is a perceived sound which is like
a bright darkness or a brightness in the dark; and this
in turn is like a sound not heard.

This paradox is probably at the farthest remove of all
from that of time and essence, but the analogies are still
clear: in so far as it is affective form, music is of the   *31*

realm of quality—that is, of essence; in so far as it is mere physical sound, it is of the realm of empirical realities, it is temporal—intrinsically so; but if the physical sound is reduced to complete silence, the essential music becomes all the more clearly audible to the spirit of the poetic idealist.

In such a reduction of the empirical reality to silence, that is, to nothing, it is a natural step to the last of the types of paradox which can be discussed here. The 'sounding silence' is, indeed, simply a special case of the more general phenomenon which may be called the paradox of 'being in non-being,' although by their very nature the two terms at times suggest a compenetration which would make them freely reversible. The starting point is the simple expression of the poet's awareness of the possible disappearance of any or all things, as they pass from being to non-being, and in this form it is not actually a paradox. In an unusually melancholy poem from *La soledad sonora,* for example, there occurs:

> Llora un clarín agudo y la luna está triste. . . ,
> grandes nubes arrastran la nueva madrugada. . . ,
> ladra un perro a las sombras, y todo lo que existe
> se hunde en el abismo sin nombre de la nada. . .
>   (*PLP* 1016)

> *A piercing clarion weeps, the moon is melancholy. . .*
> *great clouds drag off tomorrow's dawn. . . ,*
> *a dog barks at the shadows, and everything which is*
> *sinks in the nameless pit of nothingness. . .*

What keeps the concept from being a paradox is the fact that being and non-being are seen as successive rather than as simultaneous. In the later poetry, however, such simultaneity becomes very striking, as in these lines from *Poesía* on the death of the poet's mother:

¿Todo acabado, todo,
el mirar, la sonrisa;
todo, hasta lo más leve
de lo más grande?

¡No, yo sé, madre mía,
que tú, nada inmortal, un día eterno,
seguirás sonriéndome, mirándome
a mí, nada infinita! (*LP* 969)

All ended, all,
the look, the smile;
all, even what is slightest
in what is greatest?

No, mother, I know
that you, immortal nothing, one day eternal,
will always be smiling, looking
on me, an infinite nothing!

Here, then, there occurs the ultimate possible dimi-
nution of empirical and temporal existence, as the time
of a human life ends in eternal nothingness. Human
time itself is continued because another life, that of the
poet, continues its own existence, but nowhere is the
incommensurability of time and essence felt more profoundly than in such simultaneous moments of cognition: the empirical cognition of the undeniable non-ex-
istence of a beloved being and the intuitive one of an
eternal reality in that essence of personality which traditionally is called 'soul.' It is, however, not only persons that are seen to maintain such a continued reality.
We have seen previously that Juan Ramón believed his
poetic work itself would one day be " (borrada) esisten-
cia inmensa," an immense existence, even when canceled; which is to say, a reality in essence, not an empirical reality.

At times his thought on being and non-being became
even more broadly metaphysical, though never, as must

33

be constantly emphasized, more technically philosophical. A striking example of this tendency is in one of the
Romances de Coral Gables entitled "Ente":

> Se va, subiendo a lo otro.
>
> Allá arriba, donde el viento,
> sobre una raya del mundo,
> vuelo total, incandesce,
> duerme, entre piedra, sin sueño.
>
> Y los pájaros más solos
> están como para nadie,
> bajan como para todos
> al nadie que está en el todo,
> al uno que está en la nada.
> La felicidad completa:
> el ser del no ser supremo,
> el no ser del ser supremo.
>
> (*TAP* 912)

> *One goes, ascending to what is distinct.*
>
> *There, where the wind,*
> *over a boundary of the world,*
> *a total flight, is incandescent,*
> *one sleeps, amid rock, dreamlessly.*
>
> *And the loneliest birds*
> *are there as if for no one,*
> *they come down as if for everyone*
> *to the no one within the everything,*
> *to the one in the nothingness.*
> *complete felicity:*
> *the being of supreme non-being,*
> *non-being of the supreme being.*

It is known that the intuition of non-being—the fear
of death—was a source of extreme anguish for Jiménez,
and the determinant of some of the major themes
within his work. The recurring periods of emotional

34

depression which afflicted him during his entire life, from the time of his father's death in 1900 until shortly before his death in 1958, are a clear indication of his personal inability ever to subdue definitively an anguish so basic and metaphysical.[33] But in his poetry itself there occurs a definitive change from the bittersweet melancholy or dark depression of the First Period (". . . and everything which is/sinks in the nameless pit of nothingness . . .") to the serene acceptance, in the Second Period, of death and non-being as realities which are themselves a form of 'existence,' and therefore not the same as total negation. "Si 'existe' la nada," says one of the aphorisms of *Estética y ética estética* (1914–24), "¿por qué no ha de 'existir' el alma?" "If nothingness exists, why should not the soul 'exist'?" The use of quotation marks with the verb indicates that it does not refer to empirical existence but simply means 'to have reality.' At the same time, the parallel between *nada* and *alma* suggests a conception of 'soul' as the core of nothingness within an empirical being. But this, in turn, would suggest that nothingness is not absolute negation, but simply a reality whose mode of being is essential rather than empirical.

In "Ente," the poet's concern moves far beyond the individual soul to an abstract metaphysical paradise—to the beatific vision of "the being of supreme non-being,/non-being of the supreme being." The desertlike aspect of that realm of hot wind and barren rock reveals the profound sense of desolation which lies beneath the apparent serenity of the lines, but it is clear that the consolation for the poet's tragic vision of the

[33] See the biographical studies by Graciela Palau de Nemes, *Vida y Obra* (note 8 above) and Francisco Garfias, *Juan Ramón Jiménez* (Madrid, 1958).

non-being within being is the belief—of cogent plausibility for a mind so strongly inclined to think in terms of polarities, parallels, and symmetries as was Juan Ramón's—that at the heart of non-being exists a core of being, and therefore being is the only absolute.

In human terms, the perception of the non-being in being is simply the intuition of the presence of death within life. A notable instance of such an intuition occurs in a poem from *Poesía,* in which Juan Ramón asks:

> ¿Cómo, muerte, tenerte
> miedo? ¿No estás aquí conmigo, trabajando?
> ¿No te toco en mis ojos; no me dices
> que no sabes de nada, que eres hueca,
> inconciente y pacífica? . . . (*LP* 88)

> *How, death, can I fear you?*
> *Are you not here beside me, working?*
> *Do I not touch you on my eyes; do you not tell me*
> *that you taste of nothing, that you are hollow,*
> *unconscious and peaceful? . . .*[34]

So familiar, then, is the presence of death in life, that the concept of the presence of life in death becomes equally familiar and convincing, as the poem "Madre" has shown. Another striking example of the concept occurs in four brief lines from Poesía:

> Morir es sólo
> mirar adentro; abrir la vida solamente
> adentro; ser castillo inespugnable
> para los vivos de la vida. (*LP* 899)

> *To die is but*
> *to look within; to open life only*
> *within; to be a castle inexpugnable*
> *for those who live in life.*

[34] See the commentary on this poem in Howard T. Young, *The Victorious Expression* (Madison, Wisc.; 1964), pp. 113–15.

Death, then, is the ultimate ingathering of spiritual forces, but it still contains a life of its own, for the apparent tautology of the reference to "those who live in life serves to evoke the complementary concept of 'those who live in death.'

Thus, the poet has come to see that the presence of death and the void which men experience in their souls, that is, in their essential natures, does not effect a negation of their empirical existences, for men may think of death, yet continue to live; and therefore it is possible to conceive of the empirical reality of death, which awaits every man, as equally ineffective in negating the personal essences which we call souls. To state this concept of being in non-being and of life in death in terms of the contrast between time and essence with which this study of paradoxes began, it might be said that just as it is possible to conceive of things timeless and essential from within the flow of time—to think, that is, "the essential word in time"—, so it may be possible to conceive of the reality of a vital time within the realm of essences, the realm in which time itself is an essence.

The five types of paradox examined here can all be seen, then, to be analogous to and expressive of the basic one of temporality and essentiality, which Machado calls the two imperatives of poetry. By deliberately linking opposites, asserting that a thing is both minute and immense, that there are sounds both heard and not heard, that things both move and do not move, and, in patent opposition to the first principle of logic, that a thing may at the same time both be and not be—in all these ways Juan Ramón makes clear the incommensurability of the two sets of terms. He thus can save as timeless essences those values which otherwise, in the inexorable flow of time, would be carried to sure destruction. Time is, to be sure, the very substance of life (Jiménez is no less aware of this truth than is Antonio Machado), but it is also the chief problem of life, which the poet seeks to solve through his art.

It is, clearly, as metaphors that the five specific types of paradox express the fundamental one. As such they reveal a number of important aspects of the nature of the poetic art of Juan Ramón Jiménez and of the particularity he has made manifest upon the ground of the universal poetic themes of time and essence. In order to help reveal that particularity with the greatest possible clarity, it will now be necessary to analyze in greater detail the poetic forms—images, symbols, metaphors, and entire structures—by which it is expressed. The following three chapters take as their starting points certain visual forms found to be constants throughout the whole poetic work of Juan Ramón, and examine them in what is basically a chronological order. Thereby are established a series of poetic trajectories which taken together constitute a single fundamental one, that of the poet himself. This is, however, no historicism for its own sake, but an order of analysis directed toward a fuller understanding of the poetry as a whole. Rather like that of Dante, the poetry of Juan Ramón can be understood in its beginnings only from the point of view of its ultimate development, and the values of the latter can be fully felt only through a constant awareness of what had come before.

II

The exposition of the trajectories of images which concern us here will, basically, recapitulate a personal experience of reflection upon a poem encountered by chance, read *per diletto,* and inductively related to the whole of the poet's work. In such a way it is possible to set forth most clearly the basic structure of thought and sentiment within the poem and within that work as a whole. The poem is one of the most familiar of the *Arias tristes.* Since its first publication in 1903, it has been included, with variants, in all three of the poet's own anthologies and in a number of others as well. I quote the definitive version of the poem given in the *Segunda antolojía poética* and the *Tercera antolojía:*

> Viene una música lánguida,
> no sé de dónde, en el aire.
> Da la una. Me he asomado
> para ver qué tiene el parque.
>
> La luna, la dulce luna,
> tiñe de blanco los árboles,
> y, entre las ramas, la fuente
> alza su hilo de diamante.
>
> En silencio, las estrellas
> tiemblan; lejos, el paisaje
> mueve luces melancólicas,
> ladridos y largos ayes.
>
> Otro reló da la una.
> Desvela mirar el parque
> lleno de almas, a la música
> triste que viene en el aire. (*SA* 27; *TA* 51)[1]

---

[1] The original version is to be found in *LP* 265; the first revision is in *Poesías escojidas* (New York, 1917), pp. 26–27. Although this

A languid music comes—
from where I do not know—upon the air.
A clock strikes one. I have looked out
to see what the park has in it.

The moon, the gentle moon,
tinges the trees with white,
and, amid branches, the fountain
raises its thread of diamond.

In silence, the stars
tremble; far off, the horizon
moves its melancholy lights,
barking dogs, and long laments.

---

study is not generally concerned with problems of the variants in Jiménez's poetry, it is worthwhile in this case to present the earlier versions for purposes of comparison. (That of *LP* is to the left.)

Viene una música lánguida
de no sé dónde, en el aire;
da la una; me he asomado
para ver cómo está el parque.

La luna, la dulce luna
tiñe de blanco los árboles
y entre las ramas, la fuente
alza su hilo de diamante.

Las estrellas en silencio
tiemblan; lejos, el paisaje
tiene luces melancólicas,
ladridos y largos ayes.

Otro reloj da la una.
Da miedo mirar el parque
lleno de almas, a la música
triste que viene en el aire.

Viene una música lánguida,
no sé de dónde, en el aire.
Da la una. Me he asomado
para ver cómo está el parque.

La luna, la dulce luna
tiñe de blanco los árboles,
y, entre las ramas, la fuente
alza su hilo de diamante.

En silencio, las estrellas
tiemblan; lejos, el paisaje
tiene luces melancólicas,
ladridos y largos ayes.

Da la una otro reló.
Desvela mirar el parque
lleno de almas, a la música
triste que viene en el aire.

It will be seen that the total number of corrections, including those of punctuation, is quite large, although none of them changes the conceptual aspect of the poem. Nevertheless, it seems clear that the final version of the poem is the best in every way, particularly in its syntactic rhythm.

Another clock strikes one.
One stays sleepless contemplating the park,
full of souls, to the sound
of sad music on the air.

In a number of ways the poem is highly typical not only of the *Arias tristes* but of the whole of Juan Ramón's early period, which is marked by a persistent musicality and the predominance of sentiment over the intellect. Certainly both qualities are present in these lines to an unusual degree. The lilting dactyls and alliterative *l*'s, the acoustic *chiaroscuro* effected by the contrast between the dark *u*'s of line five and the sudden brightness of *tiñe* in line six, and, of course, the thematic presence of music make of the poem an almost perfect example of the expression of the musicality which is the first principle of Verlainean poetics. The emotional atmosphere is created, in typical symbolist fashion, through the "fusion of an external scene (moonlit night, silvery trees, crystal-clear water, tremulous stars) with an 'inner landscape' (solitude, sadness, sweet languor)," as Professor Diego Marín has pointed out.[2]

[2] In the notes to his anthology, *Poesía española* (México, 1958), p. 448, which are, in fact, the only commentary on the poem which I have been able to find. Cf. Émile Faguet, "Sur le Symbolisme," *Revue des Deux Mondes,* Sixième Période—LXXXIIIᵉ Année, Treizième Volume (1913), 398: "Le symbolisme, en effet, consiste à exprimer sa pensée ou son sentiment *par des allégories qui ne sont pas artificielles,* ou qui le sont le moins possible. Par exemple, un aspect de la nature, mis en parallèle avec un état d'esprit; mieux encore, une description dont on ne peut pas savoir si elle veut rendre un état de la nature ou un paysage d'âme, tant il y a de concordances entre ces deux objets: ce sont des symboles; à la condition encore qu'ils ne soient pas concertés, et qu'il soit évident ou probable que l'auteur a pensé son sentiment ou senti sa pensée ainsi et non point *traduit* ainsi sa pensée ou son sentiment."

The most notable—if not the most immediately striking—formal feature of the poem is its total structure,
which is fundamentally one of balance and symmetry.
Purely in terms of the sequence of 'events' and images,
it can immediately be seen that the last four lines repeat
what is found in the first four lines, essentially in re-
verse order. A slight variation which occurs in the reversal keeps the symmetry from being perfect—
fortunately, perhaps—but this does not alter in the least
the *impression* of symmetry which the lines convey. In
the middle stanzas there is also a certain sequential
symmetry, but much more important is the fact that
these lines depict the moon and stars overhead, the
dimly lighted background, and the silvery branches of
the trees as framing and, in a sense, enclosing, the image
which is at the center of the whole pictorial composition, the diamond thread of the fountain.

In its prosodic and acoustic aspects, too, the poem
reveals the same tendency toward symmetry. It can be
seen that the dactylic rhythm is most pronounced in the
first two and the last two lines of the poem—in both
cases associated with an explicit reference to music; that
the dactylic endings of verses in lines one, six, eleven,
and fifteen form an almost perfect pattern; and that the
previously mentioned alliteration of l's occurs in lines
equidistant from the center. Finally, there occurs in line
eight what is probably the most subtle manifestation of
the principle of symmetry in the entire poem. The vowels in this line form the sequence *aauioeiaae,* from
which we can abstract the series *aaiaa* as constituting
the really significant portion of it: the *u* and the second
i are actually semiconsonants, and the noun markers *o*
and *e* and the vowel of the preposition are so muted in
their expressiveness that their very presence in the line
is rather shadowy. If such omissions seem too arbitrary, *42*

one might count just the stressed vowels, which can scarcely be denied to stand out from the rest of the line, giving the sequence *aia*. In either case, then, there is revealed a symmetrical series in the vowels of a line which is aesthetically, if not quite mathematically, at the center of the poem, and the stressed vowel in the middle of this sequence is that of *hilo,* the diamond thread at the center of the composition.

The principle of symmetrical structure has been thoroughly integrated, then, into every aspect of the poem's form, and its effect is to suggest an intense concentration upon the central image. In spite of the pervading tone of languid melancholy, the forceful intensity of this concentration is expressed in part by the very number of concentric elements and in part by the exiguous thinness of the fountain's thread of water, the hyperbolic image of the thread suggesting that it has itself been compressed by the number of centripetal forces surrounding it. Thus it is clear that the diamond thread is much more than one of so many items in a *Stimmungsbild* of sweet melancholy; it is both qualitatively and structurally, the central image in the poem, an object of intense contemplation, an expressive symbol of great profundity. Like all expressive symbols, it shows the traits of "plurisignation" and "soft focus" characteristic of them,[3] but it is possible to give some precision to the meaning of the symbol itself and to the

[3] The terminology is borrowed from Philip Wheelwright, *The Burning Fountain: A Study in the Language of Symbolism* (Bloomington, Ind.; 1954), esp. pp. 60–75. I use the term "symbol" in the broadest sense, that is, referring to any meaningful image, whether that meaning be logical and univocal, or paradoxical and ambiguous. Thus I do not observe a distinction such as that made by Martin Foss in his *Symbol and Metaphor* (Princeton, N.J.; 1949), esp. chap. I. According to this distinction, symbol is used in connection with scientific knowledge, and anything expressing a depth meaning is called metaphor.

forma interior—as Dámaso Alonso calls it—of the poem as a whole by tracing briefly the development of the images of fountain and diamond in a number of Jiménez's later works.

For the fountain, a useful starting point is the chapter on "La fuente vieja" in *Platero y yo,* where the "plurisignation" which Jiménez himself attributes to the symbol could scarcely be greater, either in breadth or in depth. In this chapter he tells Platero that for him the fountain, like a key to a riddle or to a tomb, contains the poignancy of a cosmic lyricism, the sense of the whole truth of life. Developing this concept in detail, he adds:

> It occupies its place in such a way, such harmonious simplicity makes it eternal, color and light belong to it so completely, that one might almost be able to take from it in one's hand, as one takes its water, the stream of the whole of life. Böcklin painted it over Greece; Fray Luis translated it; Beethoven infused it with joyous tears; Michelangelo gave it to Rodin.
>
> It is the cradle and the wedding; it is the song and the sonnet; it is reality and joy; it is death.[4]

Within the multiplicity of meanings here attributed to the image, it is evident that one of the principal ones is the reference to art itself, especially to music and poetry, and the same symbolic relationship will be found at a number of points in Jiménez's poetry in verse. One of the earliest examples of an association of the fountain with music is the poem with which this chapter began, even though the relationship is one of simple concomitance and so loose that one would scarcely consider it at all symbolic. In a number of poems, however, the music is associated more in-

[4] *Platero y yo* (Buenos Aires, 1961), pp. 200-1.

trinsically with the fountain itself, as in these lines from
La soledad sonora:

> La tristeza es opaca y el amor es distante,
> las rosas de la noche piensan en lo errabundo,
> y en la fuente de bruma, el velado diamante
> canta canciones muertas de fuentes de otro mundo . . .
> (*PLP* 1008)

> *Sadness is opaque, and love is distant,*
> *the roses of the night have thoughts of errant wandering,*
> *and in the misty fountain, the veiled diamond*
> *sings dead songs of fountains of another world. . .*

More frequent, however, is the relationship of mere
juxtaposition, as, for example, in a poem to the painter
Santiago Rusiñol, written in reference to "a certain
rose" which the Catalán painter had drawn, in which
the music is the song of the nightingale:

> ¡Decoración de ensueño, ya mirada de estrellas,
> donde el surtidor, pálido, al cielo se levanta,
> mientras el ruiseñor, loco de penas bellas,
> quieto frente a la rosa que tú has pintado, canta!
> (*TA* 414)

> *Design of reverie, now looked on by the stars,*
> *where the pale jet of water rises to the sky,*
> *while the nightingale, mad with lovely sorrows,*
> *transfixed before the rose you painted, sings!*

The song poured forth from the nightingale like
water streaming from the fountain is, of course, itself a
symbol of all phenomena of creativity, including that of
the painter Rusiñol, whose name in Catalán means
'nightingale.'

Eventually, however, the association between the
fountain and music will be so close that the image will

be purely a metaphor for the sounds, as in a poem from
Belleza entitled "La música":

> De pronto, surtido
> de un pecho que se parte,
> el chorro apasionado rompe
> la sombra—como una mujer
> que abriera los balcones sollozando,
> desnuda, a las estrellas, con afán
> de un morirse sin causa,
> que fuera loca vida inmensa.
>
> Y ya no vuelve nunca más
> —mujer o agua—,
> aunque queda en nosotros, estallando
> real e inesistente,
> sin poderse parar. (*LP* 1039)

> *Sudden, the spurt*
> *of a heart that's breaking,*
> *the impassioned stream bursts through*
> *the shadow—like a woman*
> *who opened the window sobbing,*
> *naked to the stars, with longing*
> *to die without a cause,*
> *which would be an immense and frantic life.*
>
> *And then appears no more*
> *—woman or water—,*
> *although it stays within us, bursting forth*
> *real and nonexistent,*
> *and can never stop.*

The "real and nonexistent" fountain is, of course, the
metaphorical fountain, but the paradox of this phrase,
so much like that of 'being and non-being' discussed in
the previous chapter, suggests that it is also an 'essential' fountain, and that it is, consequently, in the   *46*

realm of essences that vehicle and tenor are united. Here, in fact, two vehicles in turn are presented, and their free variation (—woman or water—) with respect to the tenor suppose an essence common to all three.

When the fountain is associated with poetry, the relationship is regularly presented as being much closer. In *Platero* it was said that the old fountain *is* the sonnet, and in a brief poem inspired by Dante's *Io mi senti' svegliar* he writes that this sonnet was

> una fuente
> que dos chorros arqueaba en una taza
> primera, la cual, luego, los vertía,
> finos, en otros dos. (*LP* 631, *Eternidades*)

> *a fountain*
> *from which two streams arched out in a first basin*
> *which then poured them,*
> *in a fine stream, into another two.*

More important, however, are the instances in which the fountain symbolizes not merely the finished work but creativity itself, as when Jiménez speaks of

> el fluir de los versos constantes, en un hilo
> puro, claro, irisado, como un hilo de fuente. . .
>   (*PLP* 1083)

> *The flow of verses, constant, in a thread*
> *Pure, clear, and iridescent, like the thread of a foun-*
> *tain. . .*

In some striking lines from *Poesía* it is associated with the impetus toward expression in the exact poetic word:

¡Palabra justa y viva,
que la vida interior brota, lo mismo
que una rosa vaciada en un lucero;
cúmulo, cima del sereno monte
del corazón, contra el cenit esacto;
final estrella del surtidor recto
de la fuente más honda
—la del alma!— (*LP* 887)

Exact and living word,
which burgeons from the inner life, just like
a rose emptied within a morning star;
summit and peak of the serene mountain
of the heart, beneath the precise zenith;
final star of the upright stream
of the profoundest fountain
—of the soul!

But if in these lines the fountain symbolizes a creative projection of consciousness to the very limits of the
cosmos, it will eventually come to symbolize also a longing which transcends even these limits, just as it transcends the longing for poetic expression:

¡Ay, cómo siento el manantial,
aquí en mi corazón oscuro!
¡Ay, cuándo, como en una
fusión alta de estrella y de azucena,
ascenderá mi chorro hasta encontrar
—columna inalterable, río en pie—
el chorro derramado de lo eterno! (*LP* 854)

Oh, how I feel the spring,
here in my dark heart!
Oh, when, as in
high synthesis of flower and star,
will my fountain ascend until it meets
—unchanging column, river vertical—
the stream flowing from the eternal!

48

It is clear, then, that the fountain is used as a natural iconic symbol of transcendent longing, and it must be granted that the eternal upward flow of a fountain's jet suggests spiritual ascent as effectively and as naturally as, for example, the vertical thrust of the gothic arch.[5] But in the last line of the preceding poem the symbol acquires yet another meaning: the "chorro derramado de lo eterno" is eternity's response to human longing, an outpouring of the infinite which complements this longing and gives hope for the fulfillment of it in some indefinite future. Of particular importance, however, is the fact that the same image represents the human and the eternal—which is to say, the divine—and suggests that the search for God is basically the desire to be like God or even, perhaps, the desire to be God, the God who seeks.

There is, in any case, in the implied hope of fulfillment for human longing a clear anticipation of the mystical poetry of *Animal de fondo,* in which the infinite is at last given the name of God, and the image of the fountain will be used to describe Him as

> dios deseante y deseado,
> que surtes, desvelado
> vijilante del ocio suficiente,
> de la sombra y la luz, en pleamar fundida,
> fundido en pleamar. (*LP* 1308)

[5] With respect to the natural symbolism of the fountain, cf. the following verses from "Le Coeur de l'Eau," by Georges Rodenbach, a favorite poet of the young Jiménez:

> "Jets d'eau toujours en peine, impatients du ciel!
> Las! l'azur défia leur sveltesse de lance,
> Symbole édifiant d'une âme qui s'élance
> Et pulvérise au vent son sanglot éternel."

Oeuvres (Paris, 1923), I, 208.

> *God desiring and desired,*
> *whose stream spurts forth, the watchful*
> *guardian of the sufficient moment of reflection,*
> *from shade and light, in fused flood tide,*
> *fused in the flooding tide.*[6]

Between the composition of these lines and that of the poem of the diamond fountain at the beginning of this chapter nearly half a century had intervened, and the development in the image of the fountain is very great. From being one element in a total composition descriptive of an external scene (however imaginary), it has become a metaphor expressive of spiritual—that is, affective—forms and relationships, and it is thereby divested of every vestige of empirical reality in order better to reveal its essential reality, to 'be' nothing but its own essence. The line of development which can be traced through the points established by the several poems here quoted leads, then, from an image symbolic of a longing that becomes ever more explicitly transcendent to a metaphoric symbol of the ultimate object of longing, *id quo majus nihil cogitari potest,* conceived of as a 'person,' as 'God,' because it is not merely desired but itself desiring as well.

[6] It will be noticed that Jiménez uses a small letter rather than the capital in referring to his *dios,* clearly because he wants to distinguish his use of the name from that of traditional orthodoxy and social convention. Since there exists in English a tradition of liberal and naturalistic theology which uses the name God with the capital, into which the mystic poetry of Jiménez could easily enter, it has seemed preferable to me to translate *dios* as God rather than as god, in order to make clear that the poet is referring to the ultimate spiritual ideal rather than to a minor divinity. Apropos of this it should be pointed out that among the poems of the period of *Arte menor* (1909), are several of an apparent orthodox sentiment, in which the capital is used in addressing God as *Señor.* See Juan Ramón Jiménez, *Libros inéditos de poesía,* ed. Francisco Garfias (Madrid, 1964) pp. 86, 106, 114.

But it is necessary now to return to an earlier point on the trajectory of the fountain image to consider some lines which can also serve as a starting point for our discussion of the image of the diamond in this same poetry. Among the poems from the projected but never actually published *Arte menor* of 1909, there is one which is for our purposes particularly striking. For many years found only in the *Segunda antolojía,* it has recently been reprinted in the first volume of Jiménez's *Libros inéditos de poesía:*

> Una soledad tan pura
> como el caer de la nieve;
> un blancor divino, unánime,
> un silencio permanente. . .
>
> ¡Que todos estén muy lejos!
> ¡Que yo mismo no me acuerde
> de mí! . . .Sólo el ideal,
> con su avenida y su fuente.
>   —La fuente no saltará:
> será un éstasis perene,
> cual de un diamante atraído
> por el sinfín del poniente.

(SA 104) [7]

> *A solitude as pure*
> *as the falling of the snow;*
> *a whiteness divine, unanimous,*
> *a permanent silence. . .*
>
> *Let everyone stand far away!*
> *Let me not remember*
> *myself! Only the ideal*
> *with its avenue and fountain.*
>   *—The fountain will not leap up:*
> *it will be perennial ecstasy,*
> *like a diamond attracted*
> *by endless depth in the west.*

[7] See also *Libros inéditos,* p. 157.

Clearly present here is the familiar note of transcendent longing, a strong thrust toward the infinite,
but another important aspect of the image is its static
quality, suggesting that the scene is being contemplated
sub specie aeternitatis. The fountain of the ideal is an
"éstasis perene," and it does not leap—that is, it will
not be *seen* in motion—because it is here beheld in an
eternal contemplative moment, in which it is both as
luminous and as permanent as a diamond.[8] Obviously,
then, the diamond is a natural or iconic symbol of this
perennial ecstasy, its luminosity suggesting vision, understanding, and intellection, and its hardness symbolizing an eternal quietude, a perpetual *stasis.* The studies
of Emmy Neddermann[9] and Raimundo Lida[10] have
shown that this quality is a fundamental aspect of Jiménez's style, and its presence in the image of the diamond thread will be discussed more fully at another
point in this chapter. But one can see that the natural
symbolism of the diamond imparts this quality to any
fountain which *is* an "hilo de diamante."

The diamond is actually not a particularly frequent
image in Juan Ramón's poetry—certainly far less fre-

[8] In "El agua en la poesía de Juan Ramón Jiménez," *RHM*, V
(1939), 227, Antonio Tudisco suggested that the fountain in this
poem does not leap because it is one of those "fuentes quietas de
las cuales fluye el agua tranquila y mansamente," but I believe
the presence of the diamond in the simile justifies an interpretation of the image as not merely tranquil but completely static.
[9] *Die symbolistischen Stilelemente,* p. 4 *et passim,* and "Juan
Ramón Jiménez, sus vivencias y sus tendencias simbolistas,"
Nosotros, Segunda Época, I (1936), 20 *et passim.* In the former
work (p. 65) Miss Neddermann cites this image in our poem as
an example of the poet's preference for a substantival epithet,
de diamante, over a possible adjectival one, *diamantino,* such a
preference being itself a manifestation of a static view of the image.
This, of course, would confirm the interpretation of it based on the
intrinsic physical character of the diamond.
[10] "Sobre el estilo de Juan Ramón Jiménez," in his *Letras his-
pánicas* (México, 1958), p. 169 *et passim.*

quent than the ever-present gold. In the early works it is
used to describe what seem to be purely external qualities in water and in stars, as in one of the early *Rimas:*

> Sobre la oscura arboleda,
> en el trasparente cielo
> de la tarde, tiembla y brilla
> un diamantino lucero. (*PLP* 98)

> *Over the dark grove,*
> *in the transparent sky*
> *of the evening, trembles and shines*
> *the diamond of an evening star.*

Later, however, there occurs a greatly heightened
intensity of expressiveness as the diamond becomes a
metaphor for ideals of clarity and precision in attitude
and thought, as in this poem from *Estío* which suggests
that such an ideal is to be pursued by burning the dry
leaves of romantic melancholy (a frequent image in the
earlier *Arias tristes*) and leaving only the diamond of
pure intellection:

> Quememos las hojas secas
> y solamente dejemos
> el diamante puro, para
> incorporarlo al recuerdo,
> al sol de hoy, al tesoro
> de los mirtos venideros. . .

> ¡Sólo la guirnalda sola
> de nuestro infinito ensueño,
> lo ardiente, lo claro, lo áureo,
> lo definido, lo neto! (*LP* 1930)

> *Let us burn the dry leaves*
> *and leave only*
> *the pure diamond, that we may*
> *incorporate it into memory,*
> *in today's sun, in the treasure*
> *of the future myrtles. . .*

53

> *Only in the single garland*
> *of infinite longing,*
> *what is ardent and bright and golden,*
> *what is precise and clear!*

And eventually the diamond is identified with entities of cosmic dimension and import:

> El mundo, que hubiera sido,
> anoche, un gran carbón, mago,
> se trueca en un gran diamante,
> luna y sol en solo un astro. (*TA* 207)

> *The world, which would have been,*
> *last night, a great coal, magically,*
> *is turned into a great diamond,*
> *moon and sun in but one star.*

Still later the image acquires a meaning more fully
spiritual, if no less cosmic in its profundity. In *La estación total*, the poet asks:

> Tesoro de mi conciencia,
> ¿dónde estás, cómo encontrarte?

> Destellos, vetas, olores,
> tu mina por todas partes.

> Cada mañana, el anuncio
> (defraudado) del "¡quién sabe!"

> Cada noche, el "¡si será
> mi sueño el hondo diamante!"

> Pero el secreto aquí siempre
> y ¡alerta! sin revelarse. (*TA* 815)

> *Treasure of my consciousness,*
> *where are you, how to find you?*

> *Sparks, veins, and odors,*
> *your mine seems everywhere.*

54

> *Each morning, the portent*
> *(deceived) of "Who knows!"*

> *Each night, the "If my dream*
> *will be the profound diamond!"*

> *But the secret always here*
> *and—look closely!—unrevealed.*

The spiritual treasure anxiously sought in this question is represented by the diamond, and one senses that its significance here is analogous to that of images like the 'pearl of great price' in the gospel parable.

Finally, in *Animal de fondo*, the treasure so sought is found within the seeker's own consciousness:

> Tu voz de fuego blanco
> en la totalidad del agua, el barco, el cielo,
> lineando las rutas con delicia,
> grabándome con fúljido mi órbita segura
> de cuerpo negro
> con el diamante lúcido en su dentro. *(LP* 1301)

> *Your voice of white fire*
> *in the totality of water, ship, and sky,*
> *tracing the sea lanes with delight,*
> *engraving with effulgence my certain orbit*
> *of a dark form*
> *with the bright diamond within.*

But now the poet's consciousness of God is identical with his God's consciousness of him, and to this 'God achieved' he can now say,

> Dentro de tu conciencia jeneral estoy
> y soy tu secreto, tu diamante,
> tu tesoro mayor, tu ente entrañable. *(LP* 1354)

> *I am within your general consciousness,*
> *and I am your secret, your diamond,*
> *your greatest treasure, your intimate being.*

55

In this union of conscious minds, then, there is achieved the state regarded by mystics as the height of spiritual contemplation and the goal of its every intention, "where not only symbol and referend, but also knower and known, merge into one self-intentive whole."[11]

Having traced the trajectory of the diamond image in its development from visually descriptive metaphor to symbolic metaphor, one can now realize that its course runs exactly parallel to that of the fountain. It has been seen that the latter is basically a kinetic image, which comes to symbolize both man's longing for the infinite and also the eventual outpouring of a *dios deseante*. The diamond, on the other hand, is a static image symbolic of the ecstatic moment of luminous intellection, and yet it too is ultimately identified with God—God as knower.

What, now, of the fountain of the diamond thread? By itself it might seem, like so many other diamond images in the early poems, rather superficially descriptive, and although it is formally a metaphor, the apparent weakness of its "energy-tension"[12] would make it semantically a mere simile, at most a vague

[11] Wheelwright, *The Burning Fountain,* p. 61. It must be understood that in referring here to mystical contemplation I am not offering any particular interpretation of the state of the poet's consciousness or of the nature of mysticism generally. I simply accept the very evident truth that this is poetry in the mystic mode. In the final chapter of this book the inner meaning of this mode for Juan Ramón will be studied in greater detail.

[12] Martin Foss, *Symbol and Metaphor,* p. 60, uses this term to designate the quality of the relationship between images combined in the metaphor. A discussion of the differences between formal and semantic aspects of the simile and the metaphor is found in Wheelwright, (note 11 above), pp. 94–100.

Stimmungssymbol,[13] but we have already seen that in the context of the poem's structure it must be regarded as a symbol of quite a different order. It is clear that within the microcosm of the poem the diamond thread is at the center of all things, and therefore it is somehow the ultimate heart of the matter.

But an even more important kind of centrality suggested here is the temporal one. By this I mean not merely a sequential or chronological centrality (although it has been seen that this too is present and is the most immediately striking aspect of the symbolic structure), but rather a concept expressed in the symmetrically placed chimes striking the hour of one. Their chronometric individualism constitutes, in one respect, a faintly realistic note in the scene, but at the same time they suggest the opening up and expansion of a single moment of time to reveal eternity.

The theme of the opened and expanded moment will, in fact, appear in even more explicit form in later poems, such as one entitled "Hora inmensa" from the period 1911–1913, within which "parece que lo eterno se coje con la mano." (*TA* 369); 'it seems that the eternal can be caught in the hand.' Much later, in *La estación total,* Jiménez says of the faithfully returning blackbird that it

> . . . ensancha con su canto
> la hora parada de la estación viva,
> y nos hace la vida suficiente. (*LP* 1261)

[13] The term is used by Emmy Neddermann, *Die symbolistischen Stilelemente,* p. 137, in speaking of the essentially affective character of symbols in the poet's First Period. The whole purpose of the present chapter, of course, is to show that even in that early period what appears to be a purely affective symbol may contain a great deal of intellectual content.

> *. . . expands with its song*
> *the detained hour of the living season,*
> *and makes our life sufficient.*

The expanded moment is, therefore, a static moment, an "hora parada," and as the same poem makes clear in the lines immediately following these, such a moment is also eternity:

> ¡Eternidad, hora ensanchada,
> paraíso de lustror único, abierto
> a nosotros mayores, pensativos,
> por un ser diminuto que se ensancha!
> ¡Primavera, absoluta primavera,
> cuando el mirlo ejemplar, una mañana,
> enloquece de amor entre lo verde! (*LP* 1261)

> *Eternity, expanded hour,*
> *paradise of unique splendor, opened*
> *to us, larger, thoughtful beings,*
> *by a diminutive being who expands!*
> *Spring, absolute spring,*
> *when the exemplary blackbird, one morning,*
> *goes mad with love amid the green!*

At another point in *La estación total* a similar concept is expressed in an image whose luminosity suggests comparison with that of the diamond thread:

> ¡Florecer y vivir, istante
> de central chispa detenida,
> abierta en una forma tentadora;
> istante sin pasado,
> en que los cuatro puntos cardinales
> son de igual atracción dulce y profunda;
> istante del amor abierto
> como la flor!

To flower and live, an instant
of the sustained central spark,
opened in tempting form;
instant without past,
in which the four cardinal points
are of equal attraction, sweet, profound;
instant of love open
like the flower!

In comparing the image of the 'sustained spark' with the thread of diamond, it is clear that to both of them is attributed with striking emphasis the concept and quality of centrality—through structure in the fountain poem and through the explicit use of the adjective in the lines above; and it is clear that both can be considered diamond images, for a 'sustained spark' is precisely what a diamond is. The thread as such bears little resemblance to a spark, but a moment's reflection shows that the difference between the two images is simply that of the contrast between bilateral symmetry in the park scene to one of radial symmetry above (suggested especially by the compass image implicit in 'the four cardinal points').

Both structural concepts imply concentration upon the center, but the second of these does so with much greater intensity, and if the thinness of the thread suggested that concentration had effected a compression of its object, the smallness of the spark indicates a degree of concentration which is so much the greater, such being the logical ultimate development of the vision of the diamond thread. Clearly, however, the exiguousness of both images serves to enhance the feeling that their centrality is absolute, as though, like Euclidean abstractions, they had no extension whatever beyond the exact centers which they occupy. At the same time, this exiguousness in the object of such intense concentration suggests the presence of the paradox identified in the previous chapter as that of the *maximum in minimo,* the greatest spiritual value within the smallest physical limits.[14]

Moreover, in the central image of the poem which has been our starting-point, the paradox of *éstasis dinámico* is also present with particularly expressive force. In the natural symbolism of the diamond and in the suggestion of an expanded and sustained—or detained—moment, the image has a strong quality of stasis, but if the fountain itself is a symbol of spiritual and temporal *kinesis,* as it has been seen to be elsewhere, it can only be concluded that both phenomena are present in this image. Certainly the *kinesis* is present even in some of the most minute formal details of poem. Recalling that symmetrical series of vowels in line eight, the reader perceives with complete objectivity that in the contrast between the low *a*'s and the high *i* he can experience kinesthetically the ascent expressed lexically by the verb *alza.*[15] At the same time a great

---

[14] Further examples of the paradox of *maximum in minimo,* analogous to this symbolic exiguousness in Jiménez, might be seen in the "punto acuto" of Dante's symbolic vision of God, whose relation to the smallest star is in proportion to that of the smallest star to the moon *(Paradiso XXVIII)* ; cf. also the "Self" of Hindu mysticism, described in the *Chandogya Upanishad* as "smaller than a grain of rice, or a barley-corn, or a mustard-seed, or a grain of millet, or the kernel of a grain of millet." Quoted from *The Thirteen Principal Upanishads,* trans. Robert Ernest Hume (London, 1921), p. 210. Clearly, then, there exists a well-established type of transcendent symbol which represents the infinite by the infinitesimal, as though profundity of meaning varied inversely with physical size.

[15] It is, of course, a fact of the physiology of speech sounds that the *i* is produced with the tongue in the position of maximum possible height in the front position; the *a* requires the lowest

contrast in luminosity was suggested by the 'bright' *i* which rises between the relatively dark *a*'s. The result, then, is that this sequence of sounds itself suggests and unites the kinesis of the fountain and the luminous stasis of the diamond.

The image is, then, a remarkable example of the phenomenon of *éstasis dinámico,* constituting, in fact, the very symbol of it. This paradox, as has already been seen in the previous chapter, is one for which it is possible to find a number of explicit parallels in the poet's later works, a number of which can greatly aid the understanding of this poem itself. In the prose of the *Ideolojía lírica,* for example, he writes:

> There are two dynamisms: that of one who mounts a free force and rides off on it in a wild, blind gallop; and that of one who seizes that force, takes it in hand, encloses it, surrounds it, fixes it, rounds it, dominates it. Mine is the second.[16]

Clearly it is the second of these two dynamisms which is expressed in the image of this poem.

In *Animal de fondo,* there occurs in the poem "Río–mar–desierto" the image of a sea which is also a river and a desert, having both waves and dunes—that is, waves which are dunes and dunes which are waves, both of them symbols of divinity:

> A ti he llegado, riomar,
> desiertorriomar de onda y de duna,
> de simún y tornado, también, dios. . . (*LP* 1325)

---

possible middle position. The phenomenon of the 'luminosity' of vowels is a well-established principle of phonology, it being known that the front series suggests brightness in degrees corresponding to those of relative height, while the back series suggests darkness according to a similar series.

[16] Translated from Juan Ramón Jiménez, *Pájinas escojidas: prosa,* Selección de Ricardo Gullón (Madrid, 1948), p. 143.

> *I have come to you, river-sea,*
> *desert-river-sea of wave and dune,*
> *and of storm over sea and land as well, God. . .*

The God of this image gives 'movement in solidity,' and this

> . . .imajen
> de mi devenir fiel a la belleza
> se va igualando más hacia mi fin,
> fundiendo el dinamismo con el éstasis.

> . . .image
> *of my constant becoming toward beauty*
> *grows ever more equal as I near the end,*
> *fusing the dynamism with the ecstacy.*

The images which present the paradox of dynamic ecstasy are, then, like Wordsworth's "stationary blasts of waterfalls" (*Prelude,* VI, 626), inevitably and intrinsically "types and symbols of Eternity" (v. 639), but only *because* of the fusion of opposites within them. Stasis alone would merely suggest stopped time, an endless entropy. In eternity, in contrast, there is subsumed all the vitality of every moment which has ever been a living here-and-now, and in contrast to time it reveals an otherness which can be expressed only in paradox.

All of which is anticipated in the disarmingly simple and brief nocturne written nearly a half-century before the poems of *Animal de fondo.* Having traced the subsequent development of that poem's central image through a number of points in Juan Ramón's later poetry and prose, perhaps it is now possible to summarize the conceptual element which seems implicit in the poem, although in full realization of the inadequacies of any prose paraphrase. Such a summary will, of course, have the defect of putting in sharp focus what is meant to be seen in a much softer light, but such a sharpening is essential to clarity.

I suggest, then, that in its structure and imagery this brief poem states that there is a goal of luminous beauty which is absolutely central to everything in life, toward which all spiritual energy is concentrated, and in which the spirit finds ecstatic rest. It is approached within the flow of time, but once contemplated, it causes the moment of contemplation, however brief, to open wide to eternity and to become eternal itself.

For the poet himself, the channel of this spiritual energy is poetry, and it may even be suggested that the literal physical tension which is suggested as an inevitable result of the fusion of dynamism and ecstasy in the diamond thread of the fountain is itself an icon of the metaphoric 'tension' which is basic to all poetry. It has already been seen that one important aspect of the use of fountain images by Jiménez is their frequent association with the lyrical, music and poetry itself, and it is not surprising to find here the suggestion that it is pre-eminently through and within poetic creation that the spirit's energy is concentrated upon its goal.

Certainly such concentration upon an ideal of beauty is a fundamental constant in the whole of Jiménez's work, and one might even see the concentric poem as a kind of schema of his subsequent development, which, Gerardo Diego once said, "was not directed forward, nor upward, but inward."[17] It is, then, a progress into the heart of things, especially into the poet's own mind, and it is expressed in poetry which is ever more reduced to the essentials—that is, to essences, to pure poetry. As

---

[17] In 1923, in a discussion of the then recently published *Segunda antolojía poética*. Quoted by Gonzalo Sobejano, p. 350.

a poetic trajectory this progress is indistinguishable from the trajectory of Jiménez's own thought and consciousness, at the end of which the ideal beauty central to all things will be given the name of God, the "dios deseado y deseante." In the notes to *Animal de fondo,* he says,

> I wrote these poems while thinking, now in these penultimate days of life, I repeat, of what I had done in this world to find a God possible through poetry. And I thought then that the road toward a God was the same as any vocational road, mine as poetic writer, in this case; that all my poetic advance in poetry was an advance toward God, because I was creating a world of which the goal was to be a God. And I understood that the end of my vocation and of my life was what I have called this best consciousness in beauty, which is a general one, since for me everything is or can be beauty and poetry, expression of beauty. (*LP* 1343)

The concentric poem is, then, a chart and model of this "poetic advance," for its goal is a God of the conscious intellect whose locus, utlimately, is fully realized as being within:

> Esta conciencia que me rodeó
> en toda mi vivida,
> como halo, aura, atmósfera de mi ser mío,
> se me ha metido dentro.   (*LP* 1299)

> *This consciousness surrounding me*
> *in all of my lived life,*
> *as halo, aura, atmosphere of my own being,*
> *has now entered within me.*

The difference between the purely symbolic form in which the conceptual element is expressed in the concentric poem and explicit affirmations of *Animal de fondo* is, certainly, immense, but the lines of filiation are nevertheless clear. Indeed, it is only by tracing their

64

full trajectories that we can have any real understanding of these symbols, but, having done this, one
is left with the conviction that the meaning thus discovered was fully present in them all the while.

Much remains to be said about the nature of the God
who is the goal of Juan Ramón's lifelong pursuit and
about the ultimate significance of the paradoxical
syntheses discussed broadly in the previous chapter and
in terms of specific images in this one. But in order that
these analyses may be firmly based upon the evidence of
the poetry itself, it is necessary now to begin afresh,
establishing the trajectories of other images expressive
of Jiménez's aspirations as man and as poet.

III

The formal means by which Jiménez sought to achieve and express his perception of the essences which transcend temporal existences are many and varied, but none is as succinct, as 'simple' and 'synthetic'—to use his own terms—as the image of the rose,[1] and through a study of the principal meanings of that image, it becomes possible to discern with particular clarity the development of his intuitions concerning the phenomenon of essence in time. If the dynamic ecstasy synthesized by the visual conceit of the diamond fountain points to the timeless realm in which essences are to be found, the rose, both as natural phenomenon and as poetic image, directs attention primarily to essence itself.

Since the time of Sappho, at least, the rose has been pre-eminent in lyric poetry, and few images have been more abundant in Western literature or charged with a greater abundance of profound meanings.[2] In the poetry of Jiménez himself it may well be the most frequent of all images, but in spite of its multisecular literary history, a large part of which was undoubtedly familiar to him, that history virtually never provides the perspective within which his roses are seen. Having rejected the

---

[1] The terms appear in the notes to the *Segunda antolojía poética,* where the word *sencillo* is defined (p. 322) as "what is achieved with the fewest elements; that is, that which is clear, sharply outlined, synthetic, just."

[2] A comprehensive survey of the rose in Western literature, with particular emphasis upon modern British writers, is found in Barbara Seward, *The Symbolic Rose* (New York, 1960); for the origins of the symbol, see pp. 1–17 in this work.

literary allusion (with few exceptions, such as the *soledad sonora* from St. John of the Cross) along with most of the other externals of Modernism, Jiménez sees the rose without Parnassian overtones, and in his poetry the flowers are never explicitly sought, as even Machado confessed to having done, in the garden of Ronsard.[3] The roses of Jiménez are very much of the immediate experience of mind and sense—the experience of the impressionist, if one will. They are, then, roses of the present moment:

> . . . ella, sonriendo,
> entre sus rosas puras de hoy. (*LP* 349, *Diario*)

> . . . *she, smiling,*
> *amid her pure roses of today.*

They are disjoined from all history—free, that is, from every burden of the past:

> ¡Triunfo sin nombre! Una fragancia sin historia
> dan las rosas. Todo es armonía y ventura. (*SA* 112)

[3] A rose of Ronsard does, however, appear in *Platero y yo,* in a delightful passage which describes the poet and Platero as reading together, "Comme on voit sur la branche au mois de mai la rose . . ." See the Losada edition (Buenos Aires, 1939), pp. 23–24. A more immediate 'source' of the image for Jiménez is, doubtless, Albert Samain, whose accents are so often like those of the early Jiménez, as, for example, in a passage like: "Des roses! Des roses encor!/ Je les adore à la souffrance./ Elles ont la sombre attirance/ Des choses qui donnent la mort." From *Au Jardin de l'Infante* (Paris, 1912), p. 13. Another proximate source may be Francis Jammes, whom Juan Ramón associates with a rose in some lines from *Las hojas verdes,* "Tengo un libro de Francis Jammes/ bajo una rosa de la tar-/ de. El agua llora en mi cristal." (*PLP* 722.) A later influence is Yeats, whose "Rose of All the World" provides the title for a proposed anthology of poems on the rose.

68

Oh, nameless triumph! The roses give
a fragance without history. All is harmony and joy.

Their intrinsic newness and freshness is so absolute
that the past can not even be said to have predicted
their present beauty:

> ¡Sencillez divina
> que derrotas lo cierto y pones alma
> nueva a lo verdadero!
> ¡Rosa no presentida, que quitara
> a la rosa la rosa, que le diera
> a la rosa la rosa! (*LP* 446, *Diario*)

> *Divine simplicity*
> *that crumbles certainty and gives new soul*
> *to what is true!*
> *Rose unforeseen, that might take*
> *from the rose the 'rose' and give*
> *to the 'rose' the rose!*[4]

The ideal—revealed as such by the Spanish past sub-
junctives—is a pristine quality so pure that it strips
from the rose every sense of tradition, of the *déjà vu,*
and gives to it the quality of newness which alone is
authentic to it. Yet, within the present moment, its
intrinsic temporality is always felt. It is intrinsic, first of
all, because the rose is a natural symbol of frail mortality. Each one, like the rose of Calderón's *Príncipe
Constante,* is "escarmiento de la vida humana," ('moral
lesson for our human life'), and all of them find 'cradle
and tomb within a single bud.' In the early poetry of
Jiménez, this aspect of meaning is heightened by a frequent explicit association of the rose with human

---

[4] In the translation, I add single quotes to bring out the contrast
between the 'rose' as tradition, memory, and abstract concept and
the rose of the unique experience.

mortality itself, or with an outpouring of sentiment so sweetly painful as to seem mortal.[5]

Inevitably, then, and in spite of all the efforts made to free it from the weight of memory, the rose of the present moment comes to suggest also, especially in the earliest years, a poignant memory of past joys, which is evoked by "la nostalgia perfumada de las rosas" (*PLP* 866, *Elegías*), 'the perfumed nostalgia of the roses.'[6] The transient beauty of the same image may, however, direct attention toward the future, a future of doubt concerning the future being of that beauty, the anxiety of which impinges even upon the present:

> ¡Oh, qué duda, qué afán, qué insomnio,
> este no abandonar mi ilusión bella,
> este no querer más que esperar, loco,
> este no saber nada de las rosas
> de la futura primavera;
> de este presente casi cierto! (*TA* 359)

> *Oh, this doubt, anxiety, and sleepless fear,*
> *this holding to my fair illusion,*
> *this mad desire of expectancy,*
> *this knowing nothing of the roses*
> *of the future spring;*
> *or of this almost certain present!*

And yet, despite the darkness which surrounds the rose, in its past and in its future, more often it suggests a triumphant joy which is a consolation for sorrow:

> En las tardes de rosas y brisas,
> los dolores se olvidan, riendo,

[5] See *PLP* 77, 78, 116, *Rimas;* 281, *Arias;* 859, *Elegías.*
[6] See also *PLP* 89, *Rimas;* 1098, *Poemas mágicos; LP* 707, *Piedra.*

> y las penas glaciales se ocultan
> tras los ojos radiantes de fuego. *(PLP* 87, *Rimas)* [7]

> *In afternoons of roses and of breezes,*
> *sorrows disappear in laughter,*
> *and the chilling pain is hidden*
> *in eyes radiant with fire.*

Most frequently the joy is that of love, whose flower is rose, more than any other:

> Y me ha dicho no sé quién
> que el amor no es solitario,
> que sus flores son las rosas,
> sus ruiseñores los labios. *(PLP* 360, *Jardines)*

> *Some one—I do not know who—*
> *said that love is not alone,*
> *that its flowers are the roses,*
> *and its nightingales are lips.*

In the first period, the love suggested by the rose is sometimes frankly sensual, but more often, perhaps, it is chaste and spiritual.[8] In either case, this aspect of meaning in the image is the second principal source of what I have called its intrinsic temporality, for the love which is the response of desire to the sight of beauty (the Platonic definition having a universal validity) is, after all, a movement of the spirit which immediately implies a consequent movement through space and

---

[7] Cf. *PLP* 117, *Rimas; LP* 1034, *Belleza;* and, more particularly, for the rose of consolation, *PLP* 87, *Rimas;* 938, *Soledad; LP* 1223, *Estación.*
[8] See *PLP* 739, *Baladas; LP* 355, *Diario.* Sensuality in the image is exemplified in *PLP* 382, *Jardines;* 1178, *Laberinto;* 1437, *Melancolía.* The rose of purity is seen in *PLP* 594, *Jardines;* 1275, *Laberinto.*

time. Even when the literal movement is held in check by the *askesis*—as de Rougemont calls it—of holy awe for the purity of that beauty, the force of desire continues to strain against the bonds.

There comes a time, in any case, when the meaning of the rose moves beyond that of love and beauty in general to become identified with the beloved in a very specific sense. Perhaps the first clear manifestation of this is at the beginning of the *Sonetos espirituales:*

> Abril, sin tu asistencia clara, fuera
> invierno de caídos esplendores;
> mas aunque abril no te abra a ti sus flores,
> tú siempre esaltarás la primavera.
>
> Eres la primavera verdadera;
> rosa de los caminos interiores,
> brisa de los secretos corredores,
> lumbre de la recóndita ladera. (*LP* 13)

> *April, without your bright presence, would be*
> *a winter of fallen splendors;*
> *but though April may not open its flowers,*
> *you will always exalt the spring.*
>
> *You are the authentic spring;*
> *rose of the interior pathways,*
> *breeze of the secret corridors,*
> *light of the hidden mountainside.*

Although the *Sonetos* are almost completely free from personal anecdote, it can now be reasonably assumed that they, like much of the later poetry, are addressed to the beloved Zenobia Camprubí Aymar, and from the time of Juan Ramón's first acquaintance with her, the vague romanticism and diffuse sensuality of the early works begins to change into a love directed to a specific object, a *tú* whose presence will recur

72

throughout the rest of the poetic works.[9] It is true, as the lines just quoted suggest quite clearly, that the poet's love and desire go beyond the beloved herself to encompass the vast spaces lying between the rose, the object immediately at hand, and the distant "recóndita ladera," but they are now directed through the woman who becomes a kind of sacrament of total beauty, and through whom he can direct his devotion to that beauty. From this point on, love symbolized by the rose will no longer alternate, as in earlier years, between frank eroticism and chaste reverence. It acquires from the beloved herself a new quality of warm tenderness and of fresh innocence:

> ¡La sana, la sencilla;
> eres como la rosa,
> que a todo el que la huele
> regala igual aroma! (*LP* 117, *Estío*)

> *The sound one, the candid one,*
> *you are as the rose,*
> *who gives the same aroma*
> *to everyone who breathes it!*[10]

But most important in the new image of love is, doubtless, its particularity, which enables Juan Ramón, more fully than ever before, to find total beauty through a specific beauty. Although his pantheistic and

[9] Ultimately, of course, this *tú* is the God encountered in *Animal de fondo,* who in some measure is probably implicit also in the *tú* of the beloved.

[10] See also *LP* 37, *Sonetos.* As will be shown with respect to other aspects of Jiménez's poetry, the attainment of a new intuition or attitude usually does not bring about the complete abandonment of previous ones. It is true that after meeting Zenobia Camprubí the erotic ambivalence of the earlier poetry disappears, but the pantheistic self is, of course, a constant in all of the poetic work.

mystic tendencies continue to become more pronounced, he no longer must seek for union with that
total beauty through death, as, just a few years before
the *Sonetos,* he seemed to believe:

> Yo fuí palideciendo con las últimas notas. . .
> Un deseo inefable de perderme en las rosas,
> de morir, embriagaba mi alma melancólica. . .
>
> (*PLP* 1412)

> *I grew still paler with the final notes. . .*
> *Ineffable desire to lose myself in roses,*
> *to die, intoxicated my melancholy soul.*

Symbolic both of mortality and of love, the rose of
Juan Ramón is endued with an inner temporality by
the suggestion of an inexorable tide—of fatality in the
one and of desire in the other—which accompanies
these meanings. These are, of course, qualities inherent
in the natural symbolism of the rose, which the frag-
ments of poems examined thus far confirm and emphasize in some explicit way. In order, however, to see the
symbol as a real aesthetic entity within the poetry of
Juan Ramón, we must look beyond generic meanings to
consider the particular way in which the rose is
integrated into the total structure of a given poem. It is
well, then, as a single example, to consider here the
context of the symbol in a poem from the very early
Rimas (1902), which is striking in a number of ways. I
quote the version which appears in the *Tercera
antolojía poética:*

> Me he asomado por la verja
> del viejo parque desierto:
> todo parece sumido
> en un nostáljico sueño.

74

Sobre la oscura arboleda,
en el trasparente cielo
de la tarde, tiembla y brilla
un diamantino lucero.

Y del fondo de la sombra,
llega, acompasado, el eco
de algún agua que suspira,
al darle una gota un beso.

. . .Mis ojos pierdo, soñando,
en el vaho del sendero:
una flor que se moría,
ya se ha quedado sin pétalos:
de una rama amarillenta,
al aire trémulo y fresco,
una pálida hoja mustia,
dando vueltas, cae al suelo.

. . .Ramas y hojas se han movido,
no sé qué turba el misterio:
de lo espeso de la umbría,
como una nube de incienso,
surje una rosa fantástica,
cuyo suavísimo cuerpo
se adivina, eterno y solo
tras mate y flotante velo.

Sus ojos clava en los míos,
y, entre las brumas huyendo,
se pierde, callada y triste,
en el irse del sendero. . .

Desde el profundo boscaje,
llega, monótono, el eco
de algún agua que responde,
al darle una gota un beso.

Y allá sobre las magnolias,
en el traslúcido cielo
de la tarde, brilla y tiembla
una lágrima lucero.

. . .El jardín vuelve a sumirse
en melancólico sueño,
y un ruiseñor, dulce y alto,
jime en el hondo silencio.   (*TA* 29–31)

I have looked in through the gate
of the old deserted park:
everything seems to be deep
in a nostalgic dream.

Over the dark groves,
in the transparent sky
of the evening, shines and trembles
a diamantine star.

And from the depths of the shadows,
comes the rhythmic echo
of water that gives a sigh
when kissed by a falling drop.

My eyes wander, dreaming,
in the haze over the path:
and a flower that was dying,
is now left without petals;
from a yellowing branch,
in the air, trembling and fresh,
a pale and faded leaf
falls, in circles, to the ground.

. . .Branches and leaves now have moved,
something stirs the mystery:
from the heaviness of shadows,
like a cloud of incense,
rises a fantastic rose,
whose body of the greatest lightness
can be glimpsed, lone and eternal,
through a smoky, floating veil.
She fixes her eyes on mine,
and, fleeing amid the mists,
is lost, sad and silent,
in the disappearing path. . .

From the depths of the forest,
comes, monotonous, the sound
of the water answering
when kissed by a falling drop.

And over the magnolias,
in the diaphanous sky
of the evening, shines and trembles
a tear of an evening star.

. . .The garden again is plunged
in the melancholy dream,
and a nightingale, sweet and lofty,
weeps within the silent depth.

The aspect of structure most immediately striking in the poem is, of course, the symmetry of the sequence of images, as it was in the poem of the diamond fountain. Here too, to be sure, the symmetry is only approximate, but the remarkable thing is that a lover of vague imprecisions (of which the poem still has many) like the young Jiménez should ever have employed so architectonic a form at all.[11] In fact, of the many hundreds of poems published in books and in the *Antolojías,* only this one and the much briefer poem from the *Arias tristes* have a form which can be considered fully symmetrical. Vaguer suggestions of the form can be found in a great many poems of the First Period—and in some later poems as well—in which a

[11] Ricardo Gullón quotes Jiménez as saying, a half-century later, "Poetry loses through architecture; through the insistence on giving it a determined form, a construction. That is what happens in Góngora. Music and poetry are not visual arts, as some people seem to believe. If a poem is written in prose, if it is written down continuously, poetry gains." *Conversaciones con Juan Ramón* (Madrid, 1958), p. 115. This conviction doubtless explains his almost exclusive use of free verse after the time of publication of the *Diario.*

repetition of the opening verses balances the end against the beginning,[12] but nowhere else is the balanced repetition of images continued to the extent which is seen here: dream/star/water/path/rose/path/water/star/dream.[13]

The immediate significance of such structuring is musical and affective. Beginning in the silence of the deserted park, the poem develops in emotional intensity through a long crescendo which culminates in the surging forth through the heavy shadows of the fantastic rose, whose disappearance in the mist is followed by a *decrescendo* which ends in profound silence. The *silencio* with which the poem closes points, in fact, to the silence which is symbolic of the nothingness following upon the poem's temporal being, and which the principle of symmetry posits as antecedent to it also; so that the concept is thereby established of the being of the poem as enclosed in a surrounding silence, that is, nothingness.

---

[12] Full symmetry can be seen also in a poem *La estación total* (*LP* 1200) which will be discussed later in this chapter, but it is so brief that its symmetry is not particularly striking. In one sense, in any case, these poems simply represent the logical extension of a procedure very nearly as old as the lyric itself, that is, the repetition at the end of a poem of the image, concept, or words with which it began. We are familiar with is as the *estribillo* of the *villancico* in Spanish poetry, and any other lyrical refrain exemplifies it, as: "Sweet Thames, run softly, till I end my song." To some extent, too, it may be said that any sort of repetition has implications similar to those here pointed out with respect to the symmetrical poems, principally the conversion of linear temporality into a continuous circle, such as occurs in the musical or poetic *rondeau*.

[13] This sequence of key words has a more precise symmetry than would be found if all the repeated elements were included. Examination of the poem itself reveals, of course, that the structure is much more complex than this, although less exactly symmetrical.

The symmetry is also the very symbol of all tendencies in art toward the centripetal, toward self-containment and self-reference, and it may even be regarded as a schema of the Aristotelian concept of the three parts of the poetic whole, the reader's sense of the 'beginningness' of the beginning and the 'finality' of the end being sharpened by the contrast between those portions of the poem's being and the adjacent nothingness to which attention is so subtly drawn.

Most important of all, of course, is the fact that the symmetry directs attention very strongly to the central image of the fantastic rose, just as the symmetrical poem of the previous chapter fixes attention upon the diamond thread of the fountain. Symmetry is to such a great extent a visual phenomenon (it would probably take many more hearings of the poem for its structure to become evident than it takes readings) that in poetry it inevitably effects, in some measure, a spatialization of time.[14] The central image thus becomes an object of atemporal contemplation, and the surrounding images are like the walls of a series of concentric *moradas* which hold the central one within the innermost recesses of the mind.

This is certainly implied, as has been seen, in the symmetry of the poem of the diamond fountain, whose threadlike jet is an object of contemplation almost painful in its intensity, but in this poem the elusiveness of the fantastic rose gives the context a strange ambiguity. For while it retains the implicit suggestion of spatial-

---

[14] A very useful discussion of modern critical thought on the aesthetics of space-time is found in the first chapter of Jackson I. Cope, *The Metaphoric Structure of Paradise Lost* (Baltimore, Md.; 1962).

ized time and of the desire to enclose and hold fast the central image, the fleeting rose immediately frustrates this desire, so that the surrounding images become mere points of reciprocal reference in the space through which it escapes. Desire, then, is centripetal, but actual movement in the poem is centrifugal.[15]

In the original version which appeared in the *Rimas*, the central image of the poem was actually a "virgen fantástica" (see *PLP* 99), and only in the revised version of the *Antolojías* does the rose appear. Referentially, of course, the two words are exactly equivalent, but clearly the elusiveness of the object is expressed with far greater effectiveness by the metaphoric and symbolic 'rose' than through direct naming of the 'maiden.'[16] Another important effect of the change can be perceived on the level of acoustic expressiveness and indicates that the substitution may have been motivated in part by Jiménez's keen feeling for the musical and kinesthetic values of speech sounds. In the line, "surje una rosa fantástica," the sequence of vowels forms a structure which is a progression through the dark back series (ú-o-ó) to the clear, sonorous, and relatively

---

[15] In a brief comment on this poem, Fernand Verhesen points out in *La Torre*, p. 99 (see chap. I, note 12 above), how the images suggest the surrounding space and calls them points of departure rather than points of reference. Given the poem's symmetry—which he does not mention—I think the mutual reference is obvious and, in fact, highly effective in suggesting a 'hollowness' through which the rose flees.

[16] The change from *virgen* to *rosa* occurs again in the revision of the *Balada* beginning, "Dios está azul . . ." (*PLP* 739; *SA* 62), which appears in the anthology, *Canción* (1936). A study of all three versions of this poem is found in Bernardo Gicovate, *La poesía de Juan Ramón Jiménez* (San Juan, Puerto Rico; 1959), pp. 129–35.

much brighter *a*-sounds which are the peak of *crescendo* for the entire poem.[17] The symmetrical structure does not enter into the very sound of this central line, as it did in the poem of the diamond fountain, precisely because the image of the rose escapes capture within the poet's vision. The pure progression suggested by the sounds themselves, describing a kind of trajectory which reaches its high point in the last accent and continues on and down in the dactylic ending, strongly reinforces, at the most fundamental (almost subliminal) level of linguistic form, the intrinsic elusiveness of the object itself. The line thus gives unusually effective expression to the Mallarméan ideal, "de créer: la notion d'un objet, échappant, qui fait défaut."[18]

The line of this escape cuts across a figure which, despite the equally linear character of the symmetrical sequence of images, is, as a total complex of images, essentially concentric. The "Parque viejo" (as the poem is entitled in its original version) is a kind of *hortus*

---

[17] Juan Ramón's feeling for acoustic expressiveness is known to be acute, but it may not be as fully recognized that this expressiveness is often much more than a vague 'musicality.' An example of complex suggestiveness in a sound sequence was pointed out in the previous chapter. In Salvador Aguado-Andreut, "En torno a un poema de la 'Antolojía poética,'" *PMLA*, LXXVII (1962), 461, it has been shown that in the line, "Por él he de ir a ti," from a brief poem in the "Pastorales" of the *Antolojía* (*TA* 99), "nos hallamos (nuestra retentiva, fraguada por el ámbito lingüístico, lo engendra) ascendiendo por los monosílabos—como si fueran peldaños." The effect of ascent as if the monosyllables were a series of steps is due, of course, to the phonetic structure of the line, in which an ascent through the front series of vowels suggests the ascent of desire.

[18] From "La Musique et les lettres," *Oeuvres complètes* (Paris, 1945), p. 647.

conclusus whose "verja" surrounds the rose as much as do the other images, even though the word itself is not repeated in the poem. The implied concentricity and the movements both centripetal and centrifugal in the poem as a whole create as it were a larger version of the form basic in the rose itself.

Within the later verse, the centripetal and centrifugal movements of this early poem are reflected and developed in the same image. At times it is the center which is emphasized, and the movement is clearly centripetal, as in this poem, representative of a period of advanced poetic *depuración:*

> Como con mariposas,
> se lleva el alma suave
> su carne estremecida
> al ocaso imborrable.
>
> Allí,
> como en el cáliz
> de una rosa de fuego
> blanco, las alas arden
> inútiles,
> y se queda en su centro,
> trasparente, divina, la inmaculada carne.
> (*LP* 1054, *Belleza*)

> *As if on wings of butterflies,*
> *the tender spirit transports*
> *its trembling flesh*
> *to the indelible west.*
>
> *There, as in the chalice*
> *of a rose of white*
> *fire, the wings burn,*
> *useless,*
> *and in the center stays,*
> *transparent and divine,*
> *the spotless flesh.*

82

More frequently, however, the image of the rose, particularly the 'open rose,' suggests a movement outward from the center toward a periphery which may, ultimately, enclose the whole of reality. The movement is an expansion of spiritual forces, which in the early poetry is that of sentiments both painful and sweet:

> ¡Oh, rosas, que en la sombra del muro abandonado
> volvéis a abrir, llorando, vuestras sangrientas hojas,
> volveos a abrir en mi corazón arruinado,
> aunque os abráis de llanto, aunque os abráis de rojas!
> (*PLP* 794, *Elegías*) [19]

> *Oh, roses, that in the shadow of the abandoned wall*
> *open again, with weeping, your blood-stained leaves,*
> *open again within my crumbling heart,*
> *although it be from weeping, bursting from your own*
> *redness!*

It may also be the image of the expansive awakening of love:

> Amor, rosa encendida,
> ¡bien tardaste en abrirte!
> La lucha te sanó,
> y ya eres invencible. (*LP* 255, *Diario*)

> *Love, rose aflame,*
> *how long you took to open!*
> *The struggle made you strong,*
> *and now you are invincible.*

Later, the sentiment is more intellectualized, more purely 'poetic.' Some verses from *Poesía,* for example, describe the tremendous effort of mind required to cast out from poetry the dead weight of gross ugliness, and

---

[19] Cf. *PLP* 479, *Jardines;* 1161, *Poemas;* 1219, *Laberinto; LP* 255, *Diario.*

when the effort has succeeded, the spirit can expand
immensely:

> Ya te rodé, canto obstinado,
> en el abismo.
> > —¡Tiempo
> ¿perdido?, piedra, de mi obra pura,
> para vencer tu fealdad grosera!—
>
> Y entre el pecho y los brazos doloridos,
> la sensación divina de una jigante rosa,
> que fué—¿cuándo?—de piedra. (*LP* 843)

> *Obstinate stone, at last I rolled you*
> *into the abyss.*
> > *—Time*
> *(wasted?), stone, from my pure work,*
> *to overcome your vulgar ugliness!*
>
> *And between the breast and the aching arms,*
> *the divine sensation of a gigantic rose,*
> *which once was (when?) of stone.*

Eventually, in response to what is clearly the ultimate
intuition of transcendence in Jiménez, the expansion
within the image will be nothing less than explosive in
its force, but of this it will be necessary to speak at a
later point in this chapter.

It has been seen that the rose of Juan Ramón contains an inner dynamism which appears in the flight
through time of its brief existence; in the beauty which
elicits—and eludes—the motion of desire; and in the
movement of sentiment and intuition toward its center
as the intimate heart of reality, or out from it to encompass the world around. In each of these movements an
intrinsic temporality is made manifest which implies, to
a greater or lesser extent, the mortality of all temporal

existences, for to Jiménez the first of these movements, that of flight through time, is the primary one, and spatial movement is significant chiefly in the temporal dimension.[20] If for Aristotle time is the 'number of movement,' for Jiménez motion is, above all, the measure of time, and from the idea of time the thought of mortality is never completely separated. In studying the temporality of the rose it has not, of course, been possible or necessary to ignore the poet's conception of it as a symbol of the essences of temporal existences, but we must now consider this conception more directly, within the particular forms by which they are expressed.

The ambiguity of the various words in the Western languages for 'essence'—part, perhaps, of their heritage from alchemy—makes the fragrance of the rose, its essence in a physical sense, a natural symbol of the pure *qualitas* of its own beauty, of its essence in an ontological sense. In a number of poems, it is through this ambiguity that Jiménez expresses his own concept of essence. Much of the earliest poetry has an atmosphere heavy with the scent of roses and jasmine, fundamental in the creation of the mood of bittersweet melancholy, but later appears a conception of the fragrance of the rose as an essence of beauty separable from the existential forms of beauty, an essence which may, in its formlessness, survive their disappearance. That conception is fully developed in these lines from *Belleza:*

---

[20] From the idea of time, the thought of mortality is never completely separated, and immediately related to the anxiety of this thought is its obverse, the anxiety for eternity, which is the basic motive of the search for essences. For a discussion of these anxieties as the central theme of Juan Ramón's poetry, see A. Sánchez-Barbudo, *La segunda época de Juan Ramón Jiménez* (Madrid, 1962).

¡Rosas, rosas al cuarto
por ella abandonado!
¡Que el olor dialogue, en esta ausencia,
con el recuerdo blanco! (*LP* 1101)

Roses, roses for the room
which she has abandoned!
Let the fragrance have dialogue, within this absence,
with the white memory!

The memory which both recalls and negates the presence of the woman finds both a parallel and a symbol in the perfume which is perceived as an emanation from the roses and regarded as so autonomous that the presence of the roses themselves may be, if not negated, ignored. Thus the fragrance itself assumes the character of a 'memory' of the roses, which, as has been shown in Chapter I, can be regarded as a perception of their essence.

But the rose may also impart its essence to forms other than its own. In a prose poem of the *Diario,* a rose held in the hand of a woman asleep in a subway train transfigures the grime and ugliness which surrounds it (*LP* 328). Elsewhere in the same book the rose, now identified with the beloved, sends forth a fragrance which in the 'immensity' of its essence is able to fill the whole of ambient space:

Te deshojé, como una rosa,
para verte tu alma,
y no la vi.
Mas todo en torno
—horizontes de tierras y de mares—,
todo, hasta el infinito,
se colmó de una esencia
inmensa y viva. (*LP* 285)

I stripped the petals from you, like a rose,
to see your soul within you,
and could not see it.
But everything around
—horizons of lands and seas—
everything, to infinity,
was filled with an essence,
immense and living.

The fact that it is only when stripped of its petals—
deprived, that is, of its form—that the essence of the
rose can be perceived, makes clear the independence of
essence from existential form and even suggests a radical opposition between them.

In other poems the contrast between the two is
presented without loss of visible form in the essence, an
effect which is far superior aesthetically to that of most
of the poems in which the ambiguity of the word evokes
the concept of a formless *esencia.* In a very remarkable
poem in *Eternidades,* the sentiment of time is expressed
with a force and profundity that seem really unsurpass-
able, but the essence of the rose (here again identified
with the beloved) remains an eternal presence within
the stream of temporality:

Te siento aquí en el alma honda y clara,
cual la luz que una rosa
copiara sólo de ella
en una agua corriente. . .
Ni te lleva a las otras ellas de ella,
ni, al irte tú a otras tú, te borras.
Estás, eterna, en su inmanencia,
igual en lo sin fin de tu mudanza,
en lo sin fin de su mudanza,
cual el sol que una rosa
copiara sólo de ella en la corriente. (*LP* 638)

I feel you here in my soul, deep and bright,
like the light which a rose

might copy of itself alone
within a running water. . .
It neither bears you from itself to other selves,
nor, as you go to other selves, is your form lost.
You are, eternal, in its immanence,
the same within your endless change,
within its endless change,
like the sun which a rose
might copy from itself in running water.

Here, then, is a new symbol of essence in the rose and in the woman: the reflection of the flower in the current. It is seen, that is, within a realm of being in which it is of necessity separated from its palpable form and therefore fully as much abstracted from it as fragrance is from a flower. Such abstraction is demanded by the poem's basic and apparently paradoxical concept: that the rose within the stream is eternal, while the one rooted in the earth must inevitably disappear.

Some pages later in *Eternidades*, the essential rose is made visible in a form even more fragile than that of the reflection:

¡Sentí que lo más puro
se me cuajaba en su alegría,
cual si esa rosa que el rocío yerto
hace en la rosa suave,
la suplantara para siempre! (*LP* 660)

I felt that what was purest
condensed for me upon her joy,
as if that rose which rigid dew
forms on the tender rose
should forever supplant it!

Again a paradox: the rose of dew, the essential rose, is seen (within the terms of an *as if*) as replacing and surviving the existential rose, but it is clearly recognizable as the temporal version of a paradox already

88

known in Jiménez, that of representing immensity of significance through brevity of form.[21] Here it is not necessary to assert the eternity of the essence ("lo más puro") for it to be understood as implicit in the image; the extreme brevity of temporal existence in the rose of dew is directly symbolic of that eternity. The thought, therefore, is one of joy, but it is a joy tinged, perhaps, with nostalgia for the tenderness of the mortal rose in contrast to the crystallike image formed by the 'rigid dew,' the image of an eternal essence.

There are, on the other hand, moments when essences conceived as 'inner realities' fail to satisfy the poet, and we find him then asserting the primacy of forms. For a brief time near the end of his First Period he actually seems to regard all essences as purely illusory, and even the roses become mere convexities devoid of inner meaning:

> Todo lo que parece sin fin, duda y termina. . . ;
> el anhelo quisiera prolongar lo finito,
> y se excede a sí propio, y sobre lo que fina
> alza la cumbre de oro de otro falso infinito. . .
> ¡No! La ilusión acaba. . . Sólo las envolturas
> hacen soñar en formas hondas y prodigiosas. . . ;
> se desnuda la idea: las magias más oscuras
> surgen en una estéril convexidad de rosas. . .
> *(LP* 1436 *Melancolía)*

> *All that appears endless falls into doubt and ends. . . ;*
> *longing strives to prolong the finite,*
> *and exceeds itself, and over what has ended*
> *it raises the heap of gold of a new false infinity. . .*
> *¡No! The illusion ends. . . Only the surfaces*
> *make one dream of deep prodigious forms. . . ;*
> *the idea is denuded: the most obscure magic*
> *arises in a sterile convexity of roses. . .*

---

[21] See the discussion of this type of paradox in chap. I.

Almost at once, however, Jiménez seems to have realized that the only real error is in ignoring completely the beauty immediately at hand as he looks beyond it toward the ultimate ideal:

> ¿De qué es entonces, alma, el ansia de ideales
> lejanos que consume tus pensativas horas?
> Esa vida que ves detrás de tus cristales,
> ¿no es la vida que ríes y la vida que lloras?
>   No ansíes más ocasos, más nortes. Guarda y cuida
> tu corazón eterno entre sus rosas bellas.
>
> (PL 1437, Melancolía)

> *Of what, then, soul, is the anxiety for distant*
> *ideals which consumes your pensive hours?*
> *That life you see beyond your windows,*
> *is it not life that makes you smile and weep?*
> *No longer yearn for sunsets and the distant star.*
> *Guard and keep*
> *your heart amid its own fair roses.*

Doubt and error are dispelled by turning from the distant periphery in toward the center and from the unknown beauties beyond the horizon to those which are present here and now. This does not mean that Jiménez will from now on be a poet of objects; the transcendent urge soon reasserts itself, and the sunset will again tempt him to project his spirit beyond all human limits in the later poetry.[22]

But, although the poetry of Juan Ramón will never again show the doubt so evident in the lines quoted above, there remains with him the realization that however far fantasy may transcend the surfaces of reality, it must repeatedly return to them for its inspiration. He

---

[22] See, for example, the poetry from the section entitled "En el otro costado" in *TA,* corresponding to the years 1936–42, particularly the poems on pp. 890 and 894.

will, in such a moment, affirm the primacy of object over essence, of form over the formless, as in these striking lines from *Estío:*

> ¡Luz, sé sol; sé, olor, rosa;
> melodía, sé lira;
> lira, rosa, sol, cumbre
> de mi vida! *(LP* 185) [23]

> *Light, be the sun; fragrance, be the rose;*
> *melody, be the lyre;*
> *lyre, rose, sun, climax*
> *of my life!*

In such a moment he also rejects the intuitions prompted by the inner movements of the spirit and looks rather for the truth which radiates from things in their objective reality:

> ¡Qué buen hijo me dió a luz
> aquella sombra! Lo que era
> luna en mutilada cruz,
> es sol en rosa primera.
>   Allí queda, en un montón,
> teatral, el romanticismo;
> fuerte, ahora, el corazón
> está mejor y es el mismo.
> ¿Recordar? ¿Soñar? ¡Querer!
> ¡Bien por la alondra de oriente!
> ¡No hay más que mirar y ver
> la verdad resplandeciente! *(LP* 105, *Estío)*

> *How fair a child was given me*
> *by that shadow! What was once*
> *moonlight on a broken cross*
> *is the sun on the first rose.*
>   *There, in a hystrionic heap,*

---

[23] See the comments on this tendency and on this poem itself in Ricardo Gullón, *Estudios,* pp. 178–80.

> *lies romanticism;*
> *strong, now, my heart is both*
> *better and the same.*
> *Remember? Dream? No, love!*
> *That is well for the lark of dawn!*
> *One has only to look to see*
> *the truth which is resplendent!*

Despite such moments as these, the search for essences becomes the dominant concern in Jiménez's poetry, and it must be remembered that the lines in which the essence of the woman-rose was discovered by stripping off the petals (*LP* 285) is of the year following the lines quoted above. In fact, there is much to indicate that it is only in his Second Period that Jiménez begins clearly and fully to conceive his task as one of searching for the essences of things rather than for indefinable transcendent goals.

To be sure, the very literal sort of abstraction which occurs when forms are actually cast aside is not the only means by which the search is carried out. More than once in the years just before and after the beginning of the poet's second period, essence is regarded as a kind of Platonic idea, the conception of which is effected by a process which is as much one of synthesis as it is of abstraction. Among the poems of the period 1910–1911, known in the *Antolojías* as *Poemas agrestes,* there is one in which the essence underlying the constant cycle of death and rebirth in a field of grain is seen in such Platonizing terms:

> De nuevo se abre el grano rico en la sombra amiga
> —cuna y tumba, almo trueque—de la tierra mojada,
> para surjir de nuevo, en otra bella espiga
> más redonda, más firme, más alta y más dorado.   *92*

Y. . . ¡otra vez a la tierra! Anhelo inestinguible,
ante la norma única de la espiga perfecta,
de una suprema forma, que eleve a lo imposible
el alma, ¡oh poesía! infinita, áurea, recta! (*TA* 211)

Again the rich grain opens in the friendly shade
—cradle and tomb, fecund exchange—of the damp
earth,
to rise again, in another fair stalk,
rounder, firmer, taller, and more golden.
And. . . once more to the earth! Inextinguishable
desire,
before the unique norm of the perfect grain,
of a supreme form that raises to impossible heights
the soul, oh, poetry! infinite, golden, ever vertical!

Analogous to this longing of particular forms to achieve the perfection of the essence (the 'unique norm') and, in part, symbolized by it, is Jiménez's own search for the ideal poetic beauty through the constant process of purification. He describes it in the prologue to the *Diario:*

The constant purification of that which is unchanging, felt in the eternal unity which binds diversity in a unit of endless harmony and permanent reinternation. In the total evening, for example, what gives beauty is the intimate heart-beat of the identical fall of night, not the varied external spectacle . . . (*LP* 203)

Understandably, however, it is the rose which proves to be the most effective image of such idealism, particularly in a brief but well-known poem occurring in *Poesía:*

Todas las rosas son la misma rosa,
¡amor! la única rosa;
y todo queda contenido en ella,
breve imajen del mundo,
¡amor! la única rosa. (*LP* 909)

93

All roses are the same rose,
love, the only rose;
and all things are contained in her,
brief image of the world,
love, the only rose.

The conceptual progression within the first two of these lines ('all roses'/ 'the same rose'/ 'the unique rose') illustrates well the process of synthesis through which the poet created and discovers the essence of things, but it is a very evident merit of the poem that the result of the process is not merely an abstract summation of all roses but an authentic 'concrete universal' as well, the "rosa única" being a kind of sacrament of all values, aesthetic and intellective. The particularity of the image is, no doubt, enhanced in Jorge Guillén's more succinct version of Jiménez's first line:

¡Oh, concentración prodigiosa!
Todas las rosas son la rosa,
Plenaria esencia universal.[24]

Oh, prodigious concentration!
All roses are the rose,
Plenary universal essence.

And perhaps it is even more so in some similar lines by Rilke which are of approximately the same period, in which the particular rose, *this* rose, is made to stand out in contrast to 'all roses':

Une rose seule, c'est toutes les roses
et celle-ci: L'irremplaçable,

---

[24] From "La Florida" in *Cántico*. The profound significance of the rose for Guillén is pointed out by Joaquín Casalduero, *Cántico de Jorge Guillén* (Madrid–New York, 1953), p. 79 *et passim*.

le parfait, le souple vocable
encadré par le texte des choses.[25]

A single rose is all roses
and this one here: the irreplaceable,
the perfect one, the supple word
framed within the text of things.

But such particularity is already present, although less emphasized, in the poem of Jiménez, and there is a special value in his progressive presentation of the concept.

For Juan Ramón himself, however, even this degree of particularity will, in a later moment, seem insufficient. In *La estación total* he makes his own explicit critique of the lines from *Poesía* in a poem entitled "Rosa íntima":

> Rosa, la rosa. . . (Pero aquella rosa. . .)
> La primavera vuelve
> con la rosa
> grana, rosa, amarilla, blanca, grana;
> y todos se embriagan con la rosa,
> la rosa igual a la otra rosa.
> ¿Igual es una rosa que otra rosa?
> ¿Todas las rosas son la misma rosa?
> Sí (pero aquella rosa. . .) (*LP* 1254)

> *Rose, the rose. . . (But that rose. . .)*
> *The spring returns*
> *with the rose*
> *scarlet, pink, yellow, white, scarlet;*

---

[25] From *Les Roses* in *Sämtliche Werke* (Frankfurt, 1956) II, 576. The lines are dated September, 1924. There also exists a remarkable—and purely coincidental) similarity between the concept in this poem and one found in a fifteenth-century English carol in which the rose is the Virgin Mary: "For in this rose conteined was/ Hevene and erthe in litel space./ *Res miranda."* Quoted by Barbara Seward, *The Symbolic Rose,* p. 24.

> *everyone is intoxicated with the rose,*
> *the rose like the other rose.*
> *Is one rose like another rose?*
> *Are all roses the same rose?*
> *Yes (but that rose. . .)*

The critique does not imply a total rejection of the earlier concept, nor total reaffirmation of existential forms, but it becomes clear, in any case, that in a survey of Jiménez's poetic world as a whole the quasi-Platonic 'idea' is only one aspect of the phenomenon of essence, rather than its fundamental expression.

Yet to the extent that these 'ideas' function as ideals, as objects of aspiration, they are of profound significance in that world, and here again one finds that the rose is the most effective image of the perfection of the ideal. Such perfection is implicit in the "rosa justa," the 'precise rose' of Sonnet 40 (*LP* 56), in a "rosa magnífica y completa" (*LP* 1021, *Belleza*), and in the juxtaposition, "Rosa completa en olor./ Sol terminante en ardor." 'Rose complete in fragrance./ Sun definitive in ardor.' (*LP* 1237, *La estación total*). But most clearly of all, it is implicit in a frequently quoted little aphoristic poem, in which the perfection symbolized by the rose is the image of perfection in poetry itself:

> ¡No le toques ya más,
> que así es la rosa! (*LP* 65, *Piedra y cielo*)
>
> *Now touch it no more,*
> *for thus is the rose!*

It is curious, of course, that a poet who was so constantly and almost compulsively engaged in the revision of his work should have been able to express so strikingly his sense of the limits which must be placed upon

96

the process of retouching a poem. Ricardo Gullón has pointed out, however, that he was well aware of the importance of retaining a touch of imperfection within the perfection of an ideal beauty, as is clearly indicated in the aphorism, "Perfecto e imperfecto, como la rosa."[26] 'Perfect and imperfect, like the rose.' In another aphorism, however, he specifically glosses the poem itself in an apparent effort to show that it does not in the least conflict with his actual creative procedure:

> Crítico de mi corazón; cuando yo digo del poema:
> No le toques ya más,
> que así es la rosa,
> es después de haber tocado el poema hasta la rosa.[27]

> *Critic of my heart; when I say of the poem:*
> *Now touch it no more,*
> *for thus is the rose,*
> *it is after having touched the poem to the rose.*

It must be granted that the apology is convincing; to say 'touch it no more' is clearly not the same as saying 'touch it not at all.'

What is clear, in any case, is that for the poet any concept of perfection must in the end point to his concern for perfection in the realm of poetry, and there is evident in Juan Ramón's constant preoccupation with the *obra*, his total poetic work, a realization that it is ultimately in poetry itself, in the universe of words, that all perfections and all essences have a possible eternal reality. Among the "Poemas impersonales" of the year 1911 is one addressed to 'a poet' with reference to 'a book not written,' in which the truth of this realization

[26] Gullón, *Estudios*, pp. 192–94.
[27] Juan Ramón Jiménez, *La colina de los chopos* (Barcelona, 1963), p. 75.

and the consequent urgency of creativity are proclaimed. The final three lines of the poem were quoted in Chapter I, but here it must be quoted in full:

> Creemos los nombres.
> Derivarán los hombres.
> Luego, derivarán las cosas.
> Y sólo quedará el mundo de los nombres,
> letra del amor de los hombres,
> del olor de las rosas.
> Del amor y las rosas,
> no ha de quedar sino los nombres.
> ¡Creemos los nombres! (*TA* 254)

> *Let us create names.*
> *Men will drift away.*
> *Then, things will follow them.*
> *There will remain only the world of names,*
> *lyric of the love of humans,*
> *of the fragrance of roses.*
> *Of love and roses,*
> *only names will remain.*
> *Let us create names!*

The essence of beauty is here suggested in a way now familiar to Jiménez's readers by the 'fragrance of roses,' which is to the flower as love is to humanity, but it is only when they are given "letra," when their music has been set to words, that they can become timeless. Later Jiménez will suggest that if the act of naming is sufficiently precise, the name will be the thing itself:

> ¡Intelijencia, dame
> el nombre esacto de las cosas!
> Que mi palabra sea
> la cosa misma,
> creada por mi alma nuevamente. (*LP* 553, *Eternidades*)

> *Intellect, give me*
> *the exact name of things!*

98

> *Let my word be*
> *the thing itself,*
> *newly created by my soul.*

The poem comes startlingly close to constituting a program for a poetry of objects, of 'things as they are,' such as developed within Spain's Generation of '36, and has continued to be prominent since the end of the Civil War. It is true that the reference to 'the thing itself, newly created by my soul,' seems to lead back into subjectivity, but the final lines of the poem ask that this exact name of things be not only 'mine' (the poet's) but also 'theirs,' and it would thus be possible to interpret "creada" as 'discovered.' The fact is, that Jiménez does not, actually, found the poetry of 'things as they are' in his own work, but it is clear that at this moment he has an intuition of the relation between word and object which points to the possibility of such a poetry. Evidently, his primary concern is with the *word,* for Jiménez could never fall into the illusion of believing that a poet can approach objects in any way but through words.

Elsewhere in *Eternidades* he asserts that this poetic word is eternal, but the permanence of this word, by means of which an essence—such as that of a rose— becomes permanent, is now likened to that of a self-sufficient permanence in the flower itself:

> ¡Palabra mía eterna!
> ¡Oh, qué vivir supremo
> —ya en la nada la lengua de mi boca—
> Oh, qué vivir divino
> de flor sin tallo y sin raíz,
> nutrida, por la luz, con mi memoria,
> sola y fresca en el aire de la vida! (*LP* 688)

> *Eternal word of mine!*
> *Oh, what supreme living*
> *—Once the tongue of this mouth has become nothing-*
> *ness—*
> *oh, what divine living*
> *in flower without stem or root,*
> *nourished, by the light, with memory,*
> *alone and fresh within the air of life!*

The immortality of the poetic word is, then, that of the flower, but so closely does the flower become identified with poetry itself that each is the vehicle for the other, in perpetual compenetration.

The very act of naming things is, of course, an abstractive one,[28] but for Jiménez the giving of verbal form to essences does not devitalize them. They are not thought of as being 'captured' in poetry but rather as being liberated, in poetry, from time. In a poem entitled "Libertador," he cries,

> ¡Con qué dificultad, tiempo,
> te voy robando tus joyas
> —¡tantas joyas, tantas!—
> tus silencios—entre carro
> y grito, entre bailoteo
> y luz agria!—
>   ¡Cómo brillan
> sobre mis mano sangrientas
> y aplastadas de las moles
> que tienen que separar,
> que soportar, que rajar,
> hasta sacar la sonrisa,
> la florecilla, la estrella,
> la lágrima, la ilusión! (*LP* 898, *Poesía*)

> *With what difficulty, time,*
> *I rob you of your jewels*

---

[28] In so far, that is, as it is a categorizing one. See Amado Alonso and Raimundo Lida, *El impresionismo*, pp. 187–88.

—so many of them, so many!—
your silences—amid carts
and shouting, amid dancing
and harsh light!—
      How they shine
upon my bloodied hands,
bruised by the clods
that they must separate
and bear, and pull apart,
until they free the smile,
the flower, the star,
the tear, the aspiration!

There are moments, it is true, in which the shadowy abstraction, a "rose of shadows and of shade," seems to be a "grey essence with no more fragrance," (*LP* 1251, *La estación total*), but most of the roses of this later poetry are aflame with a vitality that transcends temporal limitations:

¡Si no es posible que corte
la rosa de fuego, hasta
dejarla justa en los límites
que le da el reló implacable! (*LP* 839, *Poesía*)

But who can cut
the rose of flame, so as
to keep it just within the bounds
the relentless clock gives it!

The rose of the later poetry is very frequently one of fire, and the poet's desire to capture this effulgent flower is as keen as it was in the melancholy young poet who longed to pursue the "rosa fantástica," but its very nature makes pursuit impossible:

—¡Cójela, coje la rosa!
—¡Que no, que es el sol!
La rosa de llama,

la rosa de oro,
la rosa ideal.
—¡Que no, que es el sol! (*LP* 1200, *La estación total*)

—*Catch it, catch the rose!*
—*Oh, no, it's the sun!*
The rose of flame,
the rose of gold,
the ideal rose.
—*Oh, no, it's the sun!*

If possession as such is impossible, there is, nevertheless, an eventual fusion of poet and rose in a flame
which liberates both of them from time and releases the
rhythms of a dance of light held captive, until then, in
potentiality:

Así danzamos juntos hacia arriba
una danza de luz que nos quedaba
(rosa, hombre, algo más) de aquel destino,
y que yo tuve el sino de librar
de su espera, que pudo ser perpetua,
(¡y qué angustia pensarlo ahora, vida!)
un ritmo dentro que salió en la llama,
inmanencia del fin de los secretos. (*TA* 941)[29]

So we danced together, moving upward,
a dance of light that was left us
(rose, man, and something more) of that destiny,
and which I had the fortune once to free
from its waiting, which might have been eternal,
(and what anguish to think that now, oh life!)
internal rhythm which came out in flame,
immanence of the end of secrets.

The flaming rose of these penultimate moments in
the poetry of Jiménez is an immediate portent of the
luminous and "unique, just, universal consciousness of

[29] The poem is from "Una colina meridiana," a section of the
Tercera antología dated 1942–50.

beauty," which in *Animal de fondo* is identified with God and symbolized by diamond, fire, or light itself.[30] In this last book the image of the rose disappears completely—except for one notable occurrence which remains to be considered. But it must be examined in the context of a summary of what has been seen of the rose thus far.

That image has proved to be so fundamental in the poetry of Jiménez that to seek out its meanings through the whole of his verse is very nearly equivalent to tracing the principal line of his entire poetic development. In studying within this image his treatment of the themes of time and essence, we have also encountered important aspects of his treatment of the phenomena of form and space, love and beauty, life and death, and the relation of all of these to art, to poetry itself. Precisely because the capacity for expressive synthesis in any literary symbol is unique to it alone, no interpretation can ever be its equivalent, but I hope that in the preceding sections of this chapter the relations of the various meanings to each other and to their common sign have been made clear. The rose is the joy of life and the sorrow of death. It is love in flesh and in spirit. It is perfect beauty in its ephemeral forms and eternal essences. And in the last instance, it is the only thing which can be fully possessed by the human spirit: a name.

There is, however, another important meaning in the symbol which derives from an intrinsic feature of the image itself, one which is common to all the roses of Juan Ramón. All of them, it can be observed, suggest a beauty of the here and now, just within reach—or just

---

[30] From the *Notas* to *Animal de fondo* (*LP* 1342).

beyond it. It is a beauty of the *más acá,* the 'here' of subjective consciousness, in confrontation with the *más allá,* the beyond, always tending toward it, yet always related implicitly to the 'here' which is that of the first person singular present implicitly or explicitly in every poem. Often the rose seems almost to be an extension of that 'I,' and sometimes even to be fully identified with it in its own encounter with the *más allá.*[31] But always it is the very image of that encounter, of the threshold between the two orders of reality.

In the notes to *Animal de fondo,* Jiménez tells us that his poetic evolution has been a successive "encounter with an idea of God," and that in three principal phases of this evolution the encounter has occurred, first, "as a mutual sensitive yielding"; then, "as an intellectual phenomenon, with accent of mutual conquest," and finally "as a discovery, as a reality of sufficient and exact truth." And he adds, "if in the first period it was ecstasy of love, and in the second avidity for eternity, in this third one it is a necessity of ambient and internal consciousness within the limits of our limited name." (*LP* 1341–42.)

Perplexing as this language may be, I believe it is possible to identify each of these stages in three poems in which the rose appears at the threshold of an encounter—an encounter which in retrospect may be understood always to have been with "an idea of God."

The first of these is addressed to a woman, who is, at the very end of the poem, subsumed into the image of a rose, which can be understood in retrospect to possess all of the qualities ascribed to the woman herself:

[31] Examples of such identification can be found in *PLP* 859, *Elegías* (and even more in the revised version of the same poem, *SA* 74), and *LP* 846, *Poesía.*

—¡Ay, mujer, más que cuerpo,
casi alma, en el punto
en que aquél va hacia ésta
y el alma es casi aquél;
jermen de confusiones
de verdad y mentira!—
¡Mujer, y no sabemos
qué dominio es el tuyo;
dónde tomar tu parte, ambigua rosa! (*LP* 860, *Poesía*)

—Oh, woman, more than body,
almost soul, at the point
in which body goes toward soul
and soul is almost body;
germ of confusion
of truth and of falsehood!—
Woman, and we do not know
which domain is yours;
where to take your part, ambiguous rose!

The exasperation and anger in these lines are clearly the sentiments of a lover, and therefore not despite but precisely because of such sentiments the poem can be considered a representative of the first phase, the phase of love and of mutual abandon within the senses. To be sure, the poem suggests that this abandon is between body and soul rather than between woman and man, but ultimately each must be implied in the other. In any case, it is clear that the ambiguous woman-rose is seen at a threshold, a point of encounter between body and soul, form and essence, *más acá* and *más allá*.

Ambiguity in this same sense can be found in another encounter, representative, I believe, of the second phase of Jiménez's evolution, that of the "intellectual phenomenon, with accent of mutual conquest." This is in a poem from *Belleza* entitled "Fuegos":

¡Este encontrarse nítido
del rayo ardiente de nuestra alma,

con el rayo imprevisto estraño; y este ser
uno la rosa—¡la esplosión!—la estrella,
en el punto inhuible
en que tocan los dos rayos vivos! (*LP* 1045)

This bright encounter
of our soul's ardent ray
with the unforeseen external ray; and this one's being
the rose—the explosion!— and the star,
in the point, inescapable,
in which touch two living rays!

The locus of the encounter between the two rays of
ardent intellection is here seen as *inhuible* (determined
by an inescapable cosmic destiny), and in this point is
the poet himself, identified with rose and star, at the
center of an explosion of intellective force which en-
compasses both elements in the encounter: "intellectual
phenomenon with accent of mutual conquest." In the
second encounter, the ray from beyond is still strange
and nameless, but it must again be remembered that it
is later understood as an encounter with God.[32]

In the poetry of *Animal de fondo,* coming at the end
of the third phase, that understanding is fully explicit.
This is the moment of the discovery of God as a "realidad de lo suficiente justo." (*LP* 1342.) The poet who
long years before had exclaimed,

[32] There is something of a problem of chronology with our first
example. The notes indicate that the end of the First Period was
when the poet was about 28 years old, and the Second when he
was almost 40, which would be in the years between 1909 and 1921.
Both poems, however, are from the 1920–1923 period. Since
Jiménez tells us that the Third Period "supone las otras dos," it is
perhaps possible that the second in some sense contains within
itself the first. The more frequent division of the works of
Jiménez into two major periods (see chap. I, note 8) is based on
criteria of style and affective tone.

¡Qué triste es amarlo todo
sin saber lo que se ama! (*PLP* 90, *Rimas*)

How sad is loving everything
without knowing what one loves!

—this same poet has now transmuted his love for an unknowable whole into a love directed to a known object, the universal consciousness within individual consciousness. It may, of course, seem strange to speak of 'univeral consciousness' as an object, for in itself it is as broad—and therefore imprecise—in meaning as the "todo" in the lines quoted above, but since it is no longer an unknowable totality, it assumes the quality of familiarity characteristic of comprehensible objects. Even more important, however, is the fact that the very act of naming the totality gives it the character of an object, even if that name be 'God.'[33]

It is within the context of this third discovery, this third encounter within the poetic trajectory of Juan Ramón, that one finds the last occurrence of the image of the rose in the published works of Jiménez—the only occurrence in *Animal de fondo*.[34] This is in the closing

[33] As in the previous chapter of this study, we find that the trajectory of one of the poet's constant images again leads to the name of God and the mystic mode of poetry in *Animal de fondo*. Thus far, it has seemed best simply to accept the poet's own language and mode of expression without presuming to pass judgment upon his actual psychic or spiritual state, but since this ultimately is what constitutes the meaning of his poetry, the following chapters will have to examine more carefully the significance of the name of God in Jiménez's last book.

[34] In the recently published poems, previously unedited, of *Dios deseado y deseante,* ed. Antonio Sánchez Barbudo, (Madrid, 1964), occur a few more images of the rose, combined—interestingly enough—with the diamond. See pp. 187, 193, and 194 of the same edition.

lines of a poem on the spiritual *patria*, "En país de países":

> ¡Qué abrirse de la boca de las rosas,
> las rosas de la boca, en estas hojas
> practicables al ojo enamorado
> que encuentra su descanso repetible
> de los dos infinitos; tan posible
> esistir, esistir mío
> en suficiente estar aquí la vida entera!
>   Un corazón de rosa construída
> entre tú, dios deseante de mi vida,
> y, deseante de tu vida, yo. (*LP* 1334)

> *What opening of the mouths of roses,*
> *the roses of the mouth, among these leaves*
> *perceptible to the enamoured eye*
> *that finds repeatable rest*
> *in both infinities; such possible*
> *existence, existence of mine*
> *in a sufficient presence of the whole of life!*
> *A heart of rose constructed*
> *between you, God desiring my life,*
> *and me, desiring your life.*

In this complex and ambiguous image, the roses of the first two lines suggest both the external, temporally limited self, in its physical and spiritual aspects (what the same poem previously calls the *cuerpialma*) , and all external forms which the self loves, as under the gaze of an inner, essential self they expand (the meaning of *abrirse* previously noted) through limitless space, thereby losing their external forms and leaving the inner self to find repose in the two infinities, of time and of space.[35] And at the heart of the inner self is

---

[35] In this implicit unification of infinite time and space, which is basically one of time *in* space, there is finally effected that spatialization of time which was suggested, more ambiguously, in some of the very earliest works of Jiménez.

found another rose, the rose of the third encounter. Symbol and sacrament of beauty in universal consciousness, this last rose is an eternal bond between the essential self and the *dios deseado y deseante,* the desired and desiring God.

Thus is achieved the ultimate fullness of meaning in an image which, once extremely abundant, has increased in intensity of significance as its occurrence has become more infrequent. In the rose of the third encounter can be found that totality of significance foreseen some twenty years previously in those lines from *Poesía* which alone can summarize a study of the rose of Juan Ramón Jiménez:

> Y todo queda contenido en ella,
> breve imajen del mundo,
> ¡amor! la única rosa.

IV

The very fact that it is possible to establish virtually continuous trajectories within Jiménez's poetry of the images of fountain, diamond, and rose is itself an indication that they are of central significance within that poetry. Yet our study of structure in the poems which were starting points in the two previous chapters has made it clear that the 'centrality' of these images is both more literal and more profoundly significant than is ever expressed in any ordinary use of the term as cliché metaphor. For it was the symmetrical structure of those poems which transformed the images into symbols of the very core of Jiménez's poetic and spiritual reality. By being placed at the center, they were subsumed into the locus of the ultimate and abiding reality of things, that is, their truth.

Particularly striking in the poem of the diamond fountain is the suggestion of 'concentration' upon the central image, and in the poem of the fantastic rose there is, in addition to such a suggestion, an implied spatialization of time which is effected through the same type of structure. But it must not be forgotten that time spatialized is still a perpetual flow—'succession,' Jiménez was to call it—and for this reason it is necessary to see the symmetry as suggesting a temporal circularity which closes off and limits the segment of time within which the poem unfolds, providing the illusion of a return to the starting point, of a successful setting apart of a circle of temporal succession tangential to time's linear advance. Every poem, to be sure, does in some sense constitute such a successful 'setting apart' by the very fact that when the experience of first reading is past it is still 'there' and can be read again and again, but the symmetrical poem adds to this the suggestion that the time of the poem is itself cyclical.

The perception of such an implication in these structures leads, then, to the realization that the symmetries which we have seen are one of the first manifestations in Jiménez's poetry of a principle of form—it is difficult as yet to speak of it as an image—of persistent recurrence and greatly varied manifestations throughout the whole of that poetry: the form of the circle or sphere. The simplest and at the same time the most 'perfect' of geometric figures, the circle has always been a symbol having a profound mystic significance; being the form of the world itself and of all celestial bodies, it is the very emblem of the infinite and the divine. In its closed, curved line, without beginning and without end, it is the model, too, for a concept of time which seeks to triumph over the irreversible linearity of our empirical experience of it. For although it is the very substance of life, time is also the chief problem of life, and the human mind, which tends to conceive it only in spatial terms, is constantly attracted by the thought that its linear succession, the inexorable flow of which carries all values to sure destruction, may be only apparently an advance straight into the unknown. The conceptual restructuring of the straight line into the circle becomes thereby a model of eternity itself, in which is preserved both the endless succession of moments and the stability of the complete and perfect form. As such, and in numerous other ways as well, it is the very image of Juan Ramón's paradox of *éstasis dinámico* and of the contradictory imperatives of temporality and essentiality. It is, however, not only in the complete form of the circumference that such stability is to be found. It is also present in the center implicit in every circle, in terms of which the circle itself is defined, and from which every circumference is generated, the smallest of them being coextensive with—and therefore identical to—the center itself. Every center, therefore, is itself an evocation of the image of the circle, as can be seen in the concept of circularity generated from the fixation upon the center in the symmetrical poems.

In this chapter, then, we must consider the principal manifestations, implicit and explicit, of the circle in the poetry of Jiménez, as well as the development of its meanings throughout the whole of his poetic trajectory. But before entering into the details of this development, it will be well to bear in mind some of the more striking aspects of the history of the circle in Western thought, in order to see Juan Ramón's use of the figure in relation to the gamut of meanings which have at other times been attributed to it, that is, in the context of its universal human significance.

At the beginning of the prologue to his history of the meaning of the circle from medieval to modern times, Georges Poulet quotes the famous definition of God from a pseudo-hermetic text of the twelfth century, the *Liber XXIV Philosophorum,* which is a useful starting point for these considerations. According to this text, *Deus est sphaera cujus centrum ubique, circumferentia nusquam.*[1] (God is a sphere whose center is everywhere, whose circumference is nowhere.) Another definition in the same text, intimately related to and immediately following the previous one, says: *Deus est totus in quolibet sui.* (God is entirely present in any part of himself.)

[1] Poulet, *Les métamorphoses du cercle,* p. 111. See chap. 1, note 27 of this study.

For our purposes, such ideas are of particular interest in so far as they give an indication of some of the ways in which the circle is associated with and expressive of logical paradox, that is, paradox composed, paradox made possible. This is even clearer in a passage from Bonaventure, in which the circle is described (as expressing the paradoxical nature of divine eternity) in terms strikingly similar to those which we have used to interpret it as a symbol of Juan Ramón's *éstasis dinámico:*

> If one says that eternity signifies an existence without end, it must be answered that one does not thereby exhaust the meaning of the word eternity; for it does not merely mean interminability, but also simultaneity; and since by the mode of interminability one must understand an intelligible circumference, without beginning and without end; so by the mode of simultaneity one must understand the simplicity and indivisibility which are the modes of the center; and these two things are affirmed at the same time of the divine Being, because He is at the same time simple and infinite; and it is thus that one must understand the circularity in eternity.[2]

In seeking, then, to comprehend these two contradictory properties of Divine Eternity, one must, as Poulet comments, in some way project the spirit in two opposite directions: "The imagination must be expanded without measure. It must also be contracted to the extreme. One must identify one's self with the immense circumference which embraces all duration *(durées)*, but also with the central point which excludes all duration."[3]

[2] *Quaestiones Disputatae, De Mysterio Trinitatis,* p. 5, art. 1, 7–8, *Opera omnia,* ed. Quaracchi, V, 91. Poulet, p. v. (The English translation is my own.)
[3] Poulet, pp. v–vi.

It is evident, then, that the uniquely constitutive property of the circle, the fact that its center is in simultaneous and equal relationship to all the points of its circumference, is the basis of its effectiveness in expressing this paradox of double movement. But this same property is what makes it expressive of the nature of divinity. In the *Vita nuova,* when Love wishes to declare his divinity to Dante, it is enough for him to say, *Ego sum tanquam centrum circuli, cui simili modo se habent circumferentiae partes; tu autem non sic.*[4] But it is the paradox which most concerns us here, for Bonaventure's pointing out the contradictory character of the properties of interminability and simultaneity gives us a close analogue of the paradox of temporality and essentiality with which this study began.

The distance—historical and cultural—between Bonaventure and Jiménez is, certainly, enormous, and although Juan Ramón's last book (and, in some sense, the whole of his poetic development) is a kind of *Itinerarium mentis in Deum,* it is unlikely that he was ever directly influenced by the Seraphic Doctor.[5] Nevertheless, since *Animal de fondo* is clearly within the mystic mode of expression, it is not surprising that the ultimate development of his use of the circle should appear—as well shall see—more like that of Bonaventure than that of intervening ages. Poulet shows that in the

---

[4] The simultaneous and equal relationship of the center to each point on the circumference is also emphasized by Aquinas, for whom it is this fact which makes the center a symbol of eternity: ". . . Centro similatur aeternitas; quae cum sit simplex et indivisibilis totum decursum temporis comprehendit et quaelibet pars temporis est ei aequaliter praesens . . ." *Declaratio quorundam Articulorum,* op. 2; quoted by Poulet, p. xxvi.

[5] Besides St. John of the Cross, the only Christian contemplative by whom Jiménez is known to have been greatly influenced is Thomas à Kempis. See Palau de Nemes, *Vida y obra,* pp. 29–31.

Renaissance there occurred a secularization of the circle whereby it came to represent the infinite range of consciousness, with the human mind—any individual mind—at the center. In the symbolist movement there again appears a spiritual version of the figure, but it is most frequently a spirituality laden with self-irony, a product of self-conscious fantasy.[6]

Jiménez is, of course, rooted in symbolism, and he may have become aware of the significance of the circle in Poe, Baudelaire, and Mallarmé; in Rilke, with whom his sensibility shows so many affinities despite the harsh criticism he occasionally made of him; in Valle-Inclán, for whom the circle is the primary symbol of the mystical aesthetics of *La lámpara maravillosa;*[7] or in his younger contemporaries, Guillén and Salinas.[8] But our concern here is not with influences in the usual sense—however interesting they may be in themselves—but rather to understand Jiménez's use of the circle on the basis of its analogies with those of the writers here quoted, who are far removed from him in time. For I believe the phenomenon must ultimately be understood, not in terms of historical influences, but rather in terms of archetypal symbolism.

Modern thought on such symbolism has, in fact, de-

---

[6] Poulet, chap. I, XIV, and XV.

[7] For the presence of the symbol in laters works of Valle-Inclán, see Jean Franco, "The Concept of Time in *El ruedo ibérico,*" *BHS*, XXXIX (1962), 177–87, and Harold L. Boudreau, "The Circular Structure of Valle-Inclán's *Ruedo ibérico,*" PMLA, LXXXII (1967), 128–35.

[8] The most explicit circle in the poetry of Salinas occurs in a poem from *Todo más claro;* see *Poesías completas* (Madrid, 1961), pp. 351–52. Jiménez doubtless read the poem, but it could certainly not have influenced his earlier work. On the circle in Guillén, see Casalduero, *Cántico de Jorge Guillén,* p. 206 *et passim.*

voted much attention to the circle. A frequently recurring image in dreams, myths, and iconic art, it is considered by Jungian psychology—which usually refers to it by the sanskrit name, *mandala*—to be a symbol of integration, of a psychic whole within which disordered multiplicity is reduced to harmonious unity.[9] And there is reason to believe that this, too, may be one important function and meaning of the circle of Juan Ramón, but of this more must be said at a later time. Our immediate concern now must be to return to the poet's work itself.

The very early poetry of Jiménez, as has often been

[9] See C. G. Jung, *The Archetypes and the Collective Unconscious,* trans. R.F.C. Hull (New York, 1959), pp. 355–90. Gilbert Durand says of the *mandala:* "Il est symbole à la puissance deux, espace sacré de poche si l'on peut dire, et qui joint à l'aspect labyrinthique les facilités de l'ubiquité. Le terme «Mandala» signifie cercle. Les traductions thibétaines en rendent l'intention profonde en le nommant «centre». Cette figure est reliée à toute une symbolique florale, labyrinthique, at au symbolisme de la maison. Il sert de «réceptacle» aux dieux, il est «palais» des dieux. Il est assimilé au Paradis au centre duquel «siège» le Dieu suprême, et dans lequel le temps est aboli par une inversion rituelle: on transforme la terre mortelle et corruptible en «terre de diamant» incorruptible, on actualise ainsi la notion de paradis terrestre. Gilbert Durand, *Les Structures anthropoliques de l'imaginaire* (Grenoble, 1960), p. 263. His reference to the *facilités de l'ubiquité* in the circle (which he explains in a later paragraph as referring particularly to the center) suggests also the archetypal character of the first pseudo-hermetic definition of God cited above *(sphaera cujus centrum ubique)*. Within Durand's own system, the circle is an archetype within the essentially feminine *Régime Nocturne* of imagery and implies a sentiment of security and "intimité féminoïde"; he criticizes Jung for interpreting it as having also the meaning of a symbol of totality, for to Durand its basic sentiment of intimacy is more a "satisfaction de suffisance qu'impérialiste mouvement de totalisation." (p. 264.) The imagery of Jiménez will show, however, that the circle can, indeed, suggest either totality achieved or, when the center has a series of rays leading from it, precisely such an "impérialiste mouvement de totalisation."

remarked, is strongly pantheistic. Sylistically it constitutes the period of Becquerian romanticism and the symbolism of Verlaine, Samain, and Rodenbach, the period of images wrapped in mist or the fading light of impressionistic landscapes. Joaquín Casalduero has pointed out that it is the particular achievement of impressionism to have found the form to express the formless,[10] and the youthful Jiménez clearly shared in this achievement to no small extent, as, for example, in these lines from the *Elegías:*

El paisaje se va de aquí hacia allá en la bruma;
el río se hace fronda, el valle se hace monte,
la primavera rosa de la tarde se esfuma
y es un otoño pálido de cerrado horizonte. (*PLP* 795)

The landscape extends from here to there, in mist;
the river becomes leaves, the valley becomes mountain,
the rosy spring of evening becomes diffused colors
and is now pale autumn of a closed horizon.

In this fascination with the blurring of lines, which in the poem quoted above leads to a Protean metamorphosis of forms, there is already a clearly implied longing for pantheistic union of the poet himself with surrounding nature, but at times that longing is made quite explicit, as in these lines from *Rimas:*

Estos crepúsculos tibios
son tan azules, que el alma
quiere perderse en las brisas
y embriagarse con la vaga
tinta inefable que el cielo
por los espacios derrama,
fundiéndola en las esencias
que todas las flores alzan
para perfumar las frentes
de las estrellas tempranas. (*PLP* 89)

[10] Casalduero, *Cántico de Jorge Guillén*, p. 141.

These balmy evenings
are so blue, that the soul
wants to be lost in the breezes
and become drunk with the vague,
ineffable tint which the sky
scatters throughout all of space,
fusing it in essences
which all the flowers lift up
to perfume the brows
of the early stars.

But this desire for fusion with the varied essences of the universe—which entails the risk of a complete dissolution and disintegration of the spirit even before the death of the body (as Hölderlin's fate warns us)—is countered by moments in which the whole of the cosmos is integrated and ordered by a structural concept which gives it unity and a basic rationality. Such a concept may, in fact, be nothing more than a line, the line of the horizon or the wall of a garden, but this is sufficient to satisfy the basic requisite of form; demarcation and limitation.

It is, however, the circle which most effectively gives order and structure to the impressionist's world of errant mists and shadows, of diffused colors and Protean shapes, and the circles implicit in the symmetrical poems studied in the two previous chapters are the first important manifestation of the form in Jiménez's poetry.[11] Such consistent symmetry as occurred there is, as

[11] Casalduero insists that the use of symmetry in the impressionists (by which he presumably means Jiménez in particular) is with an 'atmospheric' rather than a constructive intent, and that it is always in the service of the tone of melancholy and vagueness of reverie. See his *Cántico*, pp. 112–13. My contention here is fundamentally contrary to this assertion, since I regard the symmetry as intrinsically constructive, both of the affective structure of the poem and of the world which it contains.

has already been seen, really quite rare, and it is clear that Juan Ramón's thirst for transcendence constantly strains against the limits implied by such an ordering of the world. At some moments, the circle symbolizes a virtual imprisonment within all too narrow bounds. In *Melancolía*, for example, he writes:

> . . . en un rincón sin luz, sin tonos, sin fragancia;
> el pan de cada día me lo como maldito;
> como un cerco de piedra me oprime la distancia.
> (*PLP* 1428)

> . . . *in a corner without light, without tones, without fragrance;*
> *the daily bread I eat is accursed;*
> *like a hedge of stone, distance oppresses me.*

And elsewhere in the same book:

> —. . .Parece el horizonte un cinturón de hierro. . . ,
> me cansa hasta el encanto de mis propias cancio-
> nes. . . — (*PLP* 1434)

> —. . .*The horizon seems to be a belt of iron.* . . ,
> *and I am wearied even by the charm of my songs.* . . —

For a poet so strongly metaphysical as Jiménez, the sight of the horizon is normally an invitation to transcendence,[12] and when his spirit fails to respond to such an invitation, even the most sweeping vistas are oppressively confining. In these poems the circle implied in the words *cerco* and *cinturón* is clearly that of the hori-

---

[12] For example, in these lines from *Piedra y cielo:*

"Mi ciudad interior también se estiende   '*My inner city also stretches forth*
hacia el ocaso, persiguiendo   *toward the sunset, pursuing*
el caer del sol triste."   *the falling of the sad sun.*'
(*LP* 792) :

zon itself, yet even this space is too small for the restless spirit.

Many years later (in one of the lectures given in Buenos Aires in 1948), an implicit circle was the image used to express Jiménez's deeply-rooted dislike of certain kinds of poetry. In the lecture entitled "Poesía abierta y poesía cerrada," he defined 'open poetry' as marked by "huída en ansia," 'flight in anxiety,' and 'closed poetry' as "satisfacción en límite," 'satisfaction within limits.' Needless to say, it is the former which he preferred.[13] In discussing 'closed poetry,' he says, "As a boy, I felt an unbearable aversion toward the Spanish classics of the round and closed type." Round and closed, that is, circular, and implying a perfection and completeness in which the anxious spirit finds no opening for an escape to transcendence.

From the center of his horizon of consciousness, then, Juan Ramón's passion for transcendence drives him to pass beyond the limits of every circumference. Toward the end of his First Period, he writes:

> Más lejos que la gloria, que la fe, que el amor,
> que la belleza, siempre otra cosa más lejos. . .
> guirnalda que abre todas sus flores hacia allá,
> volviendo su áureo cáliz al pecho del deseo. . .
> Algo que siempre empieza en donde fina todo,
> que, sin saberse cómo, es para nuestro sueño
> cual un sueño sin forma. . . y con todas las formas. . .
> rojo si todo es blanco, débil si es todo férreo.
>
> (*PLP* 1396, *Melancolía*)

> *More distant than glory, than faith, than love,*
> *than beauty, always something else more distant. . .*
> *garland which always opens its flowers to the beyond,*
> *turning its golden chalice to the breast of desire. . .*

---

[13] *TG*, p. 96.

> *Something which always begins where everything*
> *ends,*
> *which, without one's knowing how, is for our dream*
> *like a dream without form. . . and of every form. . .*
> *red if all is white, weak if all is iron.*

And some thirty years later, in the *Romances de Coral Gables,* he will continue to seek that which is beyond every other beyond:

> Este ocaso que se apaga,
> ¿qué es lo que tiene detrás?
> ¿lo que yo perdí en el cielo,
> lo que yo perdí en el mar,
> lo que yo perdí en la tierra?
> ¿Más allá, más, más allá,
> allá que toda la tierra,
> todo el cielo y todo el mar?. . .
> ¿Más allá que yo en la nada,
> más que yo en mi nada, más
> que la nada y más que el todo
> ya sin mí, más, más allá? (*TA* 890–91)

> *This sunset which now is ending,*
> *what is the thing it keeps behind it?*
> *That which I lost in the heaven,*
> *that which I lost in the sea,*
> *that which I lost on the earth?*
> *Beyond, and ever beyond,*
> *beyond all the earth,*
> *and all the sky and sea?. . .*
> *Beyond me in nothingness,*
> *me in my nothingness, beyond*
> *nothingness itself, beyond all being*
> *now without me, still beyond?*

Gone in this later poem is the languid dissolution of the spirit in the night air which was so frequent in the earlier pantheism, and gone too is the sense of centrifugal projection symbolized, as we have seen in the previous chapter and in the lines from *Melancolía* quoted above, by the opening of the flower, but it is clear that a constant of each of these forms of transcendent longing is the implication that there is no form, no value, no sentiment in the whole of human experience which a restless fantasy cannot dream of transcending, and by the same token, every beloved object ultimately eludes the poet's grasp, leaving him, as he once put it, only with the form of its flight:

> Mariposa de luz,
> la belleza se va cuando yo llego
> a su rosa.
> Corro, ciego, tras ella. . .
> la medio cojo aquí y allá. . .
> ¡Sólo queda en mi mano
> la forma de su huída! (*LP* 777, *Piedra y cielo*) [14]

> *A butterfly of light,*
> *beauty departs when I come to its rose.*
> *Blindly, I run after her. . .*
> *I halfway seize her here and there. . .*
> *There only remains in my hand*
> *the form of her flight!*

Even in the symmetrical poems, for all the concentration on the object at the center, hemmed about as though in a *castillo interior* surrounded by a series of circular *moradas*—to use the language of Teresa of Ávila—the central image does not remain stable. The fantastic rose very clearly and explicitly escapes possession, and although the diamond fountain is more stable than the rose, it is evident that the kinesis locked in the

---

[14] The sources of the basic image and concept of this poem in St. John of the Cross and Gustavo Adolfo Bécquer have been pointed out by Howard T. Young, *The Victorious Expression* (Madison, Wisc., 1964), p. 111.

tension of the static image is not mere movement in general, but a motion directed constantly from earth to sky, from center to circumference.

There is, then, a notable ambivalence in the circle of this First Period, and one is even tempted to assert that its meaning is chiefly negative, for either it suggests imprisonment of the spirit or, in any case, something to be transcended. Nevertheless, in Jiménez's Second Period the circle continues to appear with ever greater frequency and variety in its manifestations, and ever more explicitly. In fact, even before the publication of the *Diario* there occurs in the clearly transitional book *Estío* a poem in which the circle has, in itself, a clearly positive meaning, suggesting, not confinement, but the structuring of the poet's world within a given moment, a given today. The problem which the poem records is that of projecting the structured world of today into the tomorrow, and therefore it superimposes upon the positive meaning of the circle the poet's anxiety for the future and sense of failure as the circle of 'golden truth' surrounding his subjective consciousness is broken:

> Yo no sé cómo saltar
> desde la orilla de hoy
> a la orilla de mañana.
> El río se lleva, mientras,
> la realidad de esta tarde
> a mares sin esperanza.
> Miro al oriente, al poniente,
> miro al sur y miro al norte. . .
> Toda la verdad dorada
> que cercaba al alma mía,
> cual con un cielo completo,
> se cae, partida y falsa.
> . . .Y no sé cómo saltar

124

desde la orilla de hoy
a la orilla de mañana. *(LP* 187, *Estío)* [15]

   I do not know how to leap
from the shore of today
to tomorrow's shore.
   The river carries off, meanwhile,
this evening's reality
to seas without hope.
   I look to the east, the west,
I look to the south and to the north. . .
All the gilded truth
that circled my soul,
as with a complete heaven,
falls, broken and false.
   And I do not know how to leap
from the shore of today
to tomorrow's shore.

But in the *Diario de un poeta recién casado* the circle takes on a new significance as the kind of failure recorded in the previous poem is overcome. Jiménez's sea voyage to the United States in the winter of 1916 was a profoundly moving experience for him, both in its human and personal aspect (the ship was carrying him to Zenobia Camprubí and to their eventual marriage in New York) and with respect to the significance which the ocean acquired for him as a symbol of being—being at the most profound level of experience. The *Diario*

---

[15] Basilio de Pablos, *El tiempo en la poesía de Juan Ramón Jiménez* (Madrid, 1965), pp. 126–27, points out the similarity between Jiménez's idea of the projection of being from one day to the next as a kind of voluntaristic 'leap,' and the concept of the 'leap' in Kierkegaard and Heidegger, especially the latter's idea of *Dasein's* leap from one 'now' to another. It is a difficult to understand, though, how the author of that study can assert that the verbal expression itself was actually taken by Jiménez from Heidegger, since the poem in question dates from 1915.

which he kept of the journey in verse and prose presents
a number of examples of poems in which the circle
suggests a successful establishment of order in the spiritual experience of a given moment, as in the poem,
"Tarde en ninguna parte," 'Afternoon nowhere':

> . . . ¡Este istante
> de paz—sombra despierta—,
> en que el alma se sume
> hasta el nadir del cielo de su esfera!
>   ¡Este istante feliz, sin nueva dicha,
> como un lago de oro
> rodeado de miserias!
>   ¡Este istante infinito—cielo abajo—
> entre una larga y lenta
> ola del corazón—despierta sangre—
> y una antigua, olvidada
> y nuevamente vista estrella! (*LP* 223)

> . . .*This instant*
> *of peace—awakened shadow—*
> *in which the soul sinks* **down**
> *as far as the nadir of the heaven of its sphere!*
>   *This instant of happiness, with no new joy,*
> *like a lake of gold*
> *surrounded by miseries!*
>   *This infinite instant—heaven downward—*
> *between a long and slow*
> *wave of the heart—awakened blood—*
> *and an old, forgotten*
> *and newly seen star!*

It is true that there are still moments when the circle
of the horizon on the North Atlantic is oppressively
monotonous, and in one poem it becomes clear that the
monotony is due precisely to the fact that the world
contained in the circle of each given moment is identical to every other one, so that the anxiety seen in the
poem from *Estío* concerning the difficulty of projecting

today's circle of order into tomorrow is replaced by a sense of boredom with the monotonous sameness of the successive horizons:

> El mar de olas de cinc y espumas
> de cal, nos sitia
> con su inmensa desolación.
>   Todo está igual—al norte,
> al este, al sur, al oeste, cielo y agua—
> gris y duro,
> seco y blanco.
>   Las horas son de igual medida
> que todo el mar y todo el cielo
> gris y blanco, seco y duro;
> cada una es un mar, y gris y seco,
> y un cielo, duro y blanco. (*LP* 244)

> *The sea with waves of zinc and foam*
> *of lime, surrounds us*
> *with its immense desolation.*
>   *All is the same—to the north,*
> *to the east, to the south, to the west, sky and water—*
> *grey and hard,*
> *dry and white.*
>   *The hours are of equal measure,*
> *equal to the whole sea and the whole sky,*
> *grey and white, dry and hard;*
> *each one is a sea, and grey and dry,*
> *and a sky, hard and white.*

If each passing hour is itself a sea and sky, it must also be itself a circular horizon surrounding the subjective consciousness and completely closed off from every other one. Here, then, as in the poem from *Estío,* we see the establishment of a concept in Jiménez of a circle of the moment—hour or day—radically disjoined from every other such circle, and in the early years of the Second Period, the concept seems to have been a fairly frequent one. At times it appears that he accepted such disjoining as an ideal of life and art, so that among the

aphorisms of his *Estética y ética estética* (1914–1924),
he could write:

Let us enclose ourselves in the definitive circle of each instant, and let us pass from instant to instant, as from world to world.[16]

Even more striking, perhaps, is a poem in *Piedra y cielo* which is an apology for his practice in those years of writing a great many poems in very brief lyric forms. The practice has already been mentioned in our discussion in Chapter 1 of the paradox of *maximum in minimo,* but the explanation of it given in the letter to Luis Cernuda quoted there is quite distinct from that in this poem:

> Canción corta; cortas, muchas;
> horas, horas, horas, horas
> —estrellas, arenas, yerbas,
> ondas—horas, luces; horas,
> sombras; horas de las vidas,
> de las muertes de mi vida . . .   (*LP* 782)

> *Brief song; brief ones, many;*
> *hours, hours, hours, hours*
> *—stars, sands, grasses,*
> *waves—hours, lights; hours,*
> *shadows; hours of the lives,*
> *of the deaths of my life. . .*

The many brief songs correspond, then, to the innumerable hours of life—innumerable as stars, sands, or grasses—each one of which is itself a brief life, separated from the others by innumerable deaths. But despite the character of this poem as an apology, and despite the apparent statement of an ideal in the aphorism, it seems clear that the view of life as a series of

[16] *La colina de los chopos* (Barcelona, 1963), p. 111.   *128*

discrete worlds and lives is basically the result of an anxiety concerning the problem of projecting an objective world or a subjective state of being from one moment to another. In fact, it might, perhaps, be said that such a concept constitutes the very structure of the phenomenon of such anxiety.

It is understandable, therefore, that the tendency toward atomization of time should be countered in various ways by other tendencies of thought. In a poem from the *Diario* recently quoted, the "Tarde en ninguna parte," it is evident that Jiménez has begun also to form the conception of an infinity or eternity of depth which is of the moment alone, a timeless moment conceived as the center of a temporal and spatial circle in which, as in Bonaventure's image of divine eternity, the center is in an eternal and simultaneous relation with each of the successive 'moments' of the circumference and yet remains simple and undivided. There also occurs a marked tendency to seek the eternity of the moment by centering attention upon the essence common to each moment of aesthetic experience. The phenomenon is similar, clearly, to that 'Platonizing' tendency discussed in the previous chapter, and in this case its purpose is to create the possibility of integrating all of time—that is, the whole of life—into a single unified structure, the essential circle.

It is undoubtedly present in the prologue to the *Diario,* when Jiménez writes that he has recorded in that book "the islands which the prime and single marrow of the world of the instant brought up to [his] soul, soul of a traveler, bound to the center of the unique by an elastic thread of grace." (*LP* 203–4.) In this sense of a tie to the "unique," that is, that which is one and universal, there is an awareness of the unity in essence of these successive worlds and moments. Following the Prologue, there comes in this same work a quotation from a Sanskrit "Salute of the Dawn" (evidence, this of the interest in Indian literature which had led Zenobia and Juan Ramón to translate Tagore) in which the attitude is, perhaps, even clearer:

Care well for this day! This day is life, the very essence of life. In its light passing are enclosed all the realities and all the varieties of your existence: the joy of growing, the glory of action and the splendor of beauty. (*LP* 205)

It will be recalled that the anonymous twelfth-century philosopher quoted earlier in this chapter had said, *Deus est totus in quolibet sui.* (Here, obviously, the formula is '*Vita est tota in quolibet sui.*')[17]

Being moved, then, to make an abstraction of the essence—or 'idea'—common to the several worlds of the successive moments of life, Jiménez seeks a vision of a unified world and totality of life having the eternity of a perennial present and harmoniously related to the center, the innermost self.

One of the clearest expressions of the ideal is found in a brief poem from *Eternidades* in which the circle and center symbolize the relation between the self and time as that of an eternal moment of consciousness:

[17] The same concept is expressed in one of the posthumously published poems of *Dios deseado y deseante*, entitled "Este día que es toda la vida" (p. 210, in the edition of Sánchez-Barbudo previously cited). In an aphorism of the period 1920–25, there is an interesting indication of Jiménez's awareness that his effort to achieve the concept of an 'essential' day is ultimately an effort to find an essential self, uniting the separate selves of each moment of existence: "This anxiety of mine for the universal, can it be because the selves of my daily deaths, having become distinct selves—beings, things—are calling me passionately to make with me a total self?" From *La colina de los chopos*, p. 193.

> Vivo, libre,
> en el centro
> de mí mismo.
> Me rodea un momento
> infinito, con todo—sin los nombres
> aun o ya—
> ¡Eterno! (*LP* 637)

> *I live, free,*
> *in the center*
> *of my self.*
> *Surrounding me, a moment,*
> *infinite, with everything—without such names as*
> *still or already—*
> *Eternal!*

In addition to the symbolism of the circle, the poem expresses strikingly the sense of the eternal present through the rejection of both the 'still,' by which the present is related to the past and the 'already,' by which it is related to the future. Professor González Muela has recently pointed out the significance of the affirmation of precisely these two adverbs in the expression of Jorge Guillén's sense of the temporal continuum. Their negation here is perhaps a good measure of a basic difference between the two poets, although later in this chapter there will be seen a notable instance of the reappearance and reaffirmation of the 'already' in Jiménez.

Clearly, however, the circle is the principal symbolic form within the poem, its significance surpassing that of any given word or phrase, and new aspects of its significance appear in later works of the second period. Thus, in a poem in *Piedra y cielo* there occurs a conception of the circle which is neither that of the external world nor of the relation between self and world, but of the soul itself:

¡Hermosura del alma
redonda y fuerte como un muslo,
como un pecho o un hombro;
con goce en su belleza
y confianza en su vida,
para saber que acaba en sí, que tiene
su fin en sí!
    ¡Ningún atajo
a nada! ¡Nada entre ella
y la vida! Con vida suya, y centro en ella;
dispuesta, para cuando fuere,
a salir por los ámbitos sin nombre,
jirando sola, como un astro!   (*LP* 742)

Beauty of soul,
round and strong as a thigh,
as a breast or shoulder;
with joy in its beauty
and confidence in life,
to know that it ends in itself, that it has
its goal in itself!
    No short cut
to anything! Nothing between her
and life! With life of her own and center within;
ready, when the moment comes,
to go out through nameless ambiences,
revolving alone, and like a star!

The roundness which is at first that of the feminine
form embodying the grammatically feminine *alma* is, in
the second stanza, transformed into the almost completely abstract figure of center and circle, whose course
through space and time, like that of the planets, is itself
a circle. The sense of self-sufficiency is here expressed in
terms strikingly similar to those in which the circle—as
we have seen in Bonaventure—is a symbol of Divine
Eternity itself. To be sure, in so far as they come short
of positing an objective consciousness considered as divine with which the self may be identified (and the
criterion here is not whether such an objective consciousness exists, but whether the poem posits its objec-

tivity), they may simply suggest an extreme of solipsism and what the Spanish call *ensimismamiento* (in-one's-selfness), but such qualities are already sufficiently similar to that autonomy and fullness of being unto self which men have always attributed to divinity to show the direction which Jiménez's sentiments will subsequently take.[18]

For the moment we are dealing simply with the self-sufficiency of the subjective consciousness, but it is clear, in any case, that the circle is now established very positively as its symbol. On occasion it even appears that such a circle might not improperly be called infinite, if the sense of totality and of ultimate distances can be equated with infinity. Thus, we find elsewhere in *Piedra y cielo:*

> De pronto, me dilata
> mi idea,
> y me hace mayor que el universo.
>   Entonces, todo
> se me queda dentro. Estrellas
> duras, hondos mares,
> ideas de otros, tierras
> vírjenes, son mi alma.
>   Y en todo mando yo,
> mientras sin comprenderme,
> todo en mí piensa. (*LP* 810)

> *Suddenly, my idea*
> *expands me,*
> *makes me greater than the universe.*
>   *Then, everything*
> *is left within me. Hard stars,*
> *deep seas,*
> *others' ideas, virgin*
> *lands, all are my soul.*

[18] A similar sentiment is found in a poem from *Piedra y cielo* (*LP* 717).

> *And in all things I command,*
> *while, without understanding me,*
> *all things think within me.*

In another book of the same period, *Poesía,* there occurs a brief poem which in marked contrast to the sense of spiritual expansion in the lines just quoted, suggests a centripetal movement of the spirit, similar to the 'recollection' of the religious mystic.

> ¡Concentrarme, concentrarme,
> hasta oírme el centro último,
> el centro que va a mi yo
> más lejano,
> el que me sume en el todo! (*LP* 848)

> *Concentration, concentration,*
> *until I hear my ultimate center,*
> *the center which goes to my*
> *most distant self,*
> *the one that plunges me in the all!*

But there is a fundamental ambiguity in this "most distant self." Is it distant because of being so deep in the ultimate center, or is the poet's thought suddenly projected 'out there,' to the distant periphery, as the last line so strongly suggests? The only possible answer, I believe, is that it is both, that one must accept in the ambiguity the paradox of double movement from circumference to center and from center to circumference which was implied in the lines quoted from Bonaventure, a paradox which is based on the concept of a circle 'whose center is everywhere, whose circumference nowhere.'[19]

More than twenty years after *Poesía* (and one other

[19] This same alternation of movement from center to circumference and from circumference to center was noted in the previous chapter, the circle in that case being represented by the image of the rose.

book of the same year), Jiménez published *La estación total,* containing collected verse of the period, 1923–36. These were years of upheaval in the society around him, of bitter professional polemics, and of almost complete personal isolation, but the poems of this volume show a new height of serenity and equilibrium clearly derived from the attitude of profound contemplation which is now more intense than ever. More frequently than ever before, the circle and center appear as symbols both of this equilibrium and the contemplative concentration from which it procedes. The first poem in the collection is a declaration of the soul's break with the external world, ending with the lines:

> Desde entonces, ¡qué paz!
> no tiendo ya hacia fuera
> mis manos. Lo infinito
> está dentro. Yo soy
> el horizonte recojido.
>   Ella, Poesía, Amor, el centro
> indudable. (*LP* 1135)

> *Since then, what peace!*
> *no longer do I stretch my hands*
> *outward. The infinite*
> *is within. I am*
> *the horizon ingathered.*
>   *She, Poetry, Love, the center*
> *undoubted.*

The lines do, certainly, represent an extreme of introversion, and it is precisely because of such attitudes as this that Jiménez has been severely criticized by the 'Realist' poets of Spain's post-war years who have preferred the ideals of social poetry proclaimed (more, perhaps, than practiced) by Antonio Machado.[20] Even

[20] An example of this attitude is to be found in the anthology and historical study by José María Castellet, *Veinte años de poesía española (1939–59)* (Barcelona, 1962), pp. 21–22, 40–43,

Luis Cernuda (who once had expressed much admiration for Jiménez), in one of his last essays on the older poet professes shock that there is no trace in his poetry of the turmoil in Spain during the period represented in *La estación total* and in the years immediately following.[21] In the following chapter, it will be necessary to speak of these matters again in our discussion of Jiménez's sense of his relation to objective reality, but it may be well to suggest already that the only defense he needs is the understanding of his belief that poetry has a function entirely distinct from that of prose, as well as the reminder that in the few political opinions which he expressed (in prose), his sympathies are clearly democratic and majoritarian.

One of the longer poems in *La estación total* returns to the concept of the microcosmos of the moment, in this case the brief life span of a flower. Despite the

and 49–56. The ideal of social poetry in Machado is given its best known expression in the Prologue to the second edition (1919) of his *Soledades*. To be sure, Jiménez still has numerous defenders, both within and outside of Spanish literary circles. One of the foremost of these is Ricardo Gullón, from whom it is well to quote a brief passage which very ably interprets the existential meaning of the aestheticism of the whole group of Spanish symbolists (called *modernistas*) of which Jiménez was the undisputed leader: "La convicción de que la poesía, la obra, es el último baluarte, el último reducto invulnerable del ser (contra la aniquilación) les hizo dedicarse con plenitud de esperanzas a la invención salvadora, y de ahí la paradoja del esteticismo, entendida por tantos como fuga de la vida cuando en verdad simbolizaba el ansia de afirmarla, de hacerla eterna, transmutándola en palabras imperecederas." I quote Gullón's prologue to Juan Ramón Jiménez, *El modernismo* (México, 1962), p. 24. As for Jiménez himself, he adds that it is enough to read the poet's impressions of the United States recorded in the *Diario* to see how mistaken those persons are who see the great lyric poet isolated from and different to social reality.

[21] Luis Cernuda, *Estudios sobre poesía española contemporánea* (Madrid, 1957), p. 126.

brevity of its existence, its essence (which in this poem, too, might be thought of as a Platonic idea) is eternal:

> Igual, la flor retorna
> a limitarnos el istante azul,
> a dar una hermandad gustosa a nuestro cuerpo,
> a decirnos, oliendo inmensamente,
> que lo breve nos basta.
> Lo breve al sol de oro, al aire de oro,
> a la tierra de oro, al áureo mar;
> lo breve contra el cielo de los dioses,
> lo breve en medio del oscuro no,
> lo breve en suficiente dinamismo,
> conforme entre armonía y entre luz. (*LP* 1167)

> *The same, the flower returns*
> *to limit for us the moment of blue,*
> *to give joyful fraternity to our body,*
> *to tell us, with immense fragrance,*
> *that what is brief suffices.*
> *Brevity in the sun of gold, the air of gold,*
> *the land of gold, the golden sea;*
> *brevity against the heaven of gods,*
> *brevity amid the obscure* no,
> *brevity in sufficient dynamism,*
> *conformed between harmony and light.*

Later in the same poem the circle—this time expressed in a compass image—suggests the ordering of a complete world centered about the flower and its 'instant,' that is, its span of existence, and symbolizes its 'sufficient' perpetuity. The lines have been quoted once in Chapter II, but we must examine them again:

> ¡Florecer y vivir, istante
> de central chispa detenida,
> abierta en una forma tentadora;
> istante sin pasado,
> en que los cuatro puntos cardinales
> son de igual atracción dulce y profunda;
> istante del amor abierto
> como la flor! (*LP* 1168)

To flower and live, an instant
of the sustained central spark,
opened in tempting form;
instant without past,
in which four cardinal points
are of equal attraction, sweet, profound;
instant of love, open, like the flower!

The world enclosed within this circle is that of a mere moment in the poet's experience, but for the object at the center it is the whole of life. Yet brevity of existence is regarded as sufficient not only for the flower but for all of us ("lo breve nos basta"), and therefore the spark of life at the center of the infinite circle is that which is common to each member of that 'us.' Previously, as we have seen, Jiménez has been not at all unwilling to speak explicitly of the first person singular as the center of such a circle, and the sense of plurality here is an important step toward generalization from the purely subjective sentiment. To be sure, the concept of the 'us' is not primarily that of a common humanity but simply that of 'I and other existents.' There is abundant evidence that his longing for essential being seemed to be more readily satisfied in the non-human than in human existents,[22] but it certainly could not be claimed that the "us" of this poem excludes the latter.

An even more important step toward such a pluraliz-

---

[22] The initial description of Platero, the little Andalusian donkey who was the poet's constant companion during the first part of his six years of withdrawal in Moguer (1905–11), can, I think be best understood in terms of this search for essential being: "Platero es pequeño, peludo, suave; tan blando por fuera, que se diría todo de algodón, que no lleva huesos. Solo los espejos de azabache de sus ojos son duros cual dos escarabajos de cristal negro." I quote *Platero y yo* (Buenos Aires, 1961), p. 11. The hypothetical transformation of Platero into a stuffed toy within the simile is not primarily a devitalization but simply a result of the desire to find an essence—which is, after all, the motive for all metaphors.

ing generalization is in the poem entitled "Su sitio fiel,"
in which Jiménez has made one of his most successful
efforts to achieve the ideals of "éstasis dinámico" and
intellectual lyricism:

> Las nubes y los árboles se funden
> y el sol les trasparenta su honda paz.
> Tan grande es la armonía del abrazo,
> que la quiere gozar también el mar,
> el mar que está tan lejos, que se acerca,
> que ya se oye latir, que huele ya.
> El cerco universal se va apretando,
> y ya en toda la hora azul no hay más
> que la nube, que el árbol, que la ola,
> síntesis de la gloria cenital.
> El fin está en el centro. Y se ha sentado
> aquí, su sitio fiel, la eternidad.
> Para esto hemos venido. (Cae todo
> lo otro, que era luz provisional.)
> Y todos los destinos aquí salen,
> aquí entran, aquí suben, aquí están.
> Tiene el alma un descanso de caminos
> que han llegado a su único final. (*LP* 1170)

> *The clouds and trees are fused together,*
> *and the sun shines through to them its profound peace.*
> *So great is the harmony of the embrace,*
> *that the sea wants to enjoy it as well,*
> *the sea, which is so far, and now approaches,*
> *whose pounding now we hear, whose salt air now we*
> *   smell.*
> *The universal circle now grows tighter,*
> *and now, in the blue hour, there is no more*
> *than the cloud, than the tree, than the wave,*
> *synthesis of glory at the zenith.*
> *The goal is at the center. Here reposes,*
> *as in its constant place, eternity.*
> *For this we came. (There is a falling*
> *of all other things, which were provisional light.)*
> *And all the destinies here depart,*
> *here enter, here ascend, and here they stay.*
> *The soul has then a rest from all its pathways*
> *which now have reached their single destiny.* 139

Here the synthesis of temporality and essentiality is achieved, not through any particular image such as those seen in the previous two chapters, but on a level more intimate than that of vision, through details of structure and even of grammar. In the lines,

> el mar que está tan lejos, que se acerca,
> que ya se oye latir, que huele ya,

the "ya" which was explicitly rejected in an earlier poem now marks the successive moments of the temporal dynamism and of the swelling excitement at the approach of the sea. At the same time, this successiveness is paralleled by the continuous process by which the distant circumference approaches the center: "el cerco universal se va apretando." In the three lines immediately following these the movement reaches its climax:

> y ya en toda la hora azul no hay más
> que la nube, que el árbol, que la ola,
> síntesis de la gloria cenital.

In this last line, which comes at the very center of the poem, phonetic structure again gives resonance—as it had in the early poems which began our studies of images in the two previous chapters—to the conceptual content, for the symmetrical vowel pattern *ieoei* stands out strikingly from the entire line and puts *gloria,* which we may equate with eternity, at the center of the poem.

This eternity is the fixed goal of all the previous movement, but within its fixity is the profound dynamism of movement to and from the center:

140

Y todos los destinos aquí salen,
aquí suben, aquí están.

These destinies are, in one sense, seen as the innumerable radii of the universal circle, but their constant motion suggests the image, not so much of a geometrical abstraction, as of a living thing.

From the vision which Jiménez achieved in this poem, it is but a short step to a mode of explicit mysticism which we find in his last book, *Animal de fondo.* Just as his first sea voyage in 1916 had coincided with—and in some sense caused—the fundamental change in poetic forms and in world-view which marks the beginning of his Second Period, so it was the long voyage to Argentina in 1948 which effected the short but critical step to this poetic mysticism. This time, the great circle of horizon on the sea gave striking reality to his intuition of the position of the subjective consciousness within the world of the mind. But the consciousness at the center of that circle is no longer purely subjective, and therefore it can no longer feel imprisoned, no longer alone.

The indications we have seen in the poems from *La estación total* of a developing synthesis of subject and object in Juan Ramón's concept of circle and center are brought to full fruition in *Animal de fondo,* as the eternity at the center of the circle becomes for him a *Thou,* the "God desired and desiring," with perfect union between that God and the self—perfect union, that is, between subjective and universal consciousness.[23] No better expression of that sentiment can be

[23] The appearance of *Thou* (I use the archaic English form as a brief way of referring to the concept of 'second person singular,' although in translation from the poetry I prefer to use the

found in the entire book than in the poem "Al centro rayeante," in which the 'radiant center' is identified with the *dios deseado y deseante:*

> Tú vienes con mi norte hacia mi sur,
> tú vienes de mi este hasta mi oeste,
> tú me acompañas, cruce único, y me guías
> entre los cuatro puntos inmortales,
> dejándome en su centro siempre y en mi centro
> que es tu centro. (*LP* 1302–03)

> *You come with my north toward my south,*
> *you come from my east up to my west,*
> *with me you come, the unique crossing, and guide me,*
> *within the four immortal points,*
> *leaving me ever in its center and in mine,*
> *which is your center.*

But God is not only the point coinciding with the center of subjective consciousness (not only that point and yet fully to be found in that point for anyone who accepts the hermetic maxim that *Deus est totus in quolibet sui*), he is also 'out there,' in the surrounding circle of horizon on the open sea:

> Mar desierto, con dios
> en redonda conciencia
> que me habla y me canta,
> y me confía y me asegura. . . (*LP* 1297)

---

modern 'you,' even with reference to the Divinity) is doubtless closely related to the appearance—or rather, the culminating development—of the sense of the eternal present in the final poems. These will be discussed further in the last chapter of this study. According to Martin Buber, "the real, filled present exists only in so far as actual presentness, meeting, and relation exist. The present arises only in virtue of the fact that the *Thou* becomes present." *I and Thou,* trans. Ronald Gregor Smith (2d. ed.; New York, 1958), p. 12.

> *Deserted sea, with God*
> *in circled consciousness*
> *who speaks and sings to me,*
> *confides and gives assurance.* . . *(LP* 1297)

God, then, is within the poet and he in God, that is, the self's intentional awareness of universal consciousness is directed both inward and outward, and God is found, now at the center of consciousness, as in "Al centro rayeante," now at its periphery, as in these posthumously published lines from *Dios deseado y deseante.*

> Sucesión de coronas es mi dios,
> coronas que coronan solo un centro
> que es un ojo, es un ver,
> un sí mismo tan yo, maravilloso yo,
> que mi aurora no es más que la sonrisa
> de haberme dado a luz yo mismo
> de mi sueño, mi sueño. *(DDD* 170)

> *Succession of crowns is my God,*
> *crowns which crown a single center*
> *which is an eye, a seeing,*
> *an itself that is so much I, wonderous I,*
> *that my dawn is but the smile*
> *of having brought myself to light*
> *from my sleep, from my sleep.*

The poetry of Jiménez's last years thus reveals a dimension of paradox more radical even than that of the interminability and simultaneity in the circle of Bonaventure: if God is both at the center and the circumference of consciousness, one can only conclude that, like all harmoniously paired opposites, center and circumference ultimately are one.

There is, of course, no image or figure which can

represent such an identity absolutely, the impossibility of which is precisely what leads us to speak of it as a paradox. But it is doubtless the poet's desire to suggest that identity as closely as possible which leads to the particular emphasis of some poems upon the zenith as the point to which consciousness is directed. In the sphere of the geometrician, certainly, no point of the circumference can be regarded as more directly above the center than any other, but from man's terrestrial perspective, which continues to be the model of Jiménez's spiritual landscape despite the extreme of abstraction to which his poetic *depuración* has brought him, the zenith is, clearly, the one point on the visible hemisphere which is related most directly to the center and is therefore perceived as closest to it.

Ultimately, however, such figurative approximation can never be sufficient, and therefore a more adequate expression of the union of consciousness must always be the figure which represents the actual coincidence of their symbols. We have seen this union in the coincidence of centers in circles of consciousness, but it can also occur in the circumferences. This, in fact, is an additional meaning in the lines from *Animal de fondo* quoted near the end of the previous chapter:

> ¡Qué abrirse de la boca de las rosas,
> las rosas de la boca, en estas hojas
> practicables al ojo enamorado
> que encuentra su descanso repetible
> de los dos infinitos. . . ! (*LP* 1334)

> *What opening of the mouths of roses,*
> *the roses of the mouth, among these leaves*
> *perceptible to the enamoured eye*
> *that finds repeatable rest*
> *in both infinities. . . !*

Here, as in the preceeding poem, the subjective consciousness is simply an 'eye,' not only because it is 'that which sees,' but also because it is 'that which circumscribes'—that is, because it is itself a circle, and the act of perception here implies an exact meeting or congruence of the circle of the perceiving eye with that of the expanding circle which is its object. In the poem from *Dios deseado y deseante,* the implication of congruence is not as strong, but looking back at it now with the awareness that the 'eye' must, indeed, be thought of as itself a circle, we realize that the poem's identification of the center as an eye effects an even closer approximation of center and circumference than does the directing of attention to the zenith, for that center which is itself simply an inner circle is no longer an absolute opposite of the circumference but is, rather, parallel to it.

Observing the presence within these poems of the circles which are subsumed in the images of *ojo, corona, rosa,* and *boca,* it is impossible not to reflect that these forms show also a permeation of the concept of the circle to the very material substance of Jiménez's thought—that is, to the most minute details of its linguistic form. All of the words contain the same accented vowel, one which graphically—and, in some sense, acoustically—is itself a circle, and it is impossible to believe that Jiménez's ear and eye did not perceive this.[24] Clearly, of course, it is principally in their mean-

[24] The fact that all of these Spanish nouns contain the same vowel is, in a sense, pure coincidence, but it should be clear that for a poet as conscious of sound as Jiménez it would still be a *significant* coincidence. Emmy Neddermann notes briefly that at the beginning of the poet's Second Period the vowel *o* seems to correspond to the "gedanklichen Tiefe und Schwere der späteren Erlebnisse" (p. 144), and of course these qualities always ac-

ings that the words represent consciousness—both that of the subject and that of the transcendent object—as a circle, in the coincidence of which is formed the

> . . . corazón de rosa construida
> entre tú, dios deseante de mi vida,
> y, deseante de tu vida, yo.[25]

company the appearance of the circle, so that this significance too is present in the coincidence. It is clear, in any case, that in the later poetry this vowel is sometimes so abundant that there can be no question whatsoever that it is being deliberately sought out. In a poem previously quoted from *La estación total*, the lines which center a flower in the middle of a compass image (the compass is sometimes known in Spanish, by the way, as *la rosa de los vientos*) are followed by the lines:

> "Amor y flor en perfección de forma,
> en mutuo sí frenético de olvido,
> en compensación loca;
> olor, sabor y olor,
> color, olor y tacto, olor, amor, olor." *(LP 1168)*

A similar interpretation of the significance of sound is made by Casalduero when he speaks of Guillén's use of a 'circular' rhyme in *o* to symbolize 'the instant in its plenitude.' (p. 216.)

[25] For translation of these lines, see the preceding chapter. With reference to Jiménez's use of the rose as a manifestation of the circle of eternity, it is significant that among the numerous projects for a definitive reordering of his complete poetic works was one which included the compilation of a special *Antolojía de la rosa*. Both in the papers held in the *Archivo Nacional* in Madrid, dating from before the poet's departure in 1936, and in the materials contained in the Sala Zenobia y Juan Ramón Jiménez in the library of the University of Puerto Rico, there are a number of notes relating to such a project. Those in the latter collection date from some time shortly after the death of Enrique Díez-Canedo in 1944, and are more extensive than those from the earlier period. The planned title for the anthology was *Con la rosa del mundo*, inspired, probably, by Yeats's "rose of all the world," and was to be dedicated to the memory of Díez-Canedo. Particularly interesting in the outline of the work is the chronological arrangement—or rather, rearrangement—of the poems. In the anthology *Canción* (1936), chronology had been

Here, then, as in the many other occurrences of the circle in *Animal de fondo,* the figure resolves symbolically the relation of eternity, the realm of essences, to time. For it expresses and resolves the paradox of the union of simultaneity and successiveness which the mystic regards as intrinsic in eternity and must therefore be regarded as the ultimate symbol of that paradox to which Jiménez gave the name of "éstasis dinámico."

It also organizes the whole of reality into a single meaningful form, meaningful because in contrast to the chaos of an unorganized totality of experience, form does not merely have meaning, it *is* meaning, simply because it 'makes sense.' But there is an important further development in the significance of the circle which is shown in the lines quoted from "Al centro rayeante." This title itself presents the image of a point from which issues a series of lines that are both radii of the circle and rays of light. Indeed, the neologism *rayeante* suggests much more effectively than the traditional Latinism *radiante* the literal giving off of rays, not only because it preserves the stem of *rayos* but because in the verbal suffix *-ear* and its participial *-eante* there is implied a movement of palpitation and of flickering im-

---

deliberately ignored as a result of the poet's desire to make all the poems in it 'relive' in the present moment. For the rose anthology, chronology was not abandoned, but the rearrangement of the poems made clear Jiménez's desire to reorder the linearity of time—the time both of his work and of his own life—into an infinite circle. The whole of his work was divided into seven periods, whose order in the book was to be 7,5,3,1,2,4,6, thus producing a symmetry containing an intrinsically implied circularity, reinforced, in fact, by the tension between the arbitrarily determined sequential order and natural numerical order, the latter always referring attention back to the beginning of the series.

possible to translate but highly effective in evoking the inner dynamism of the image.

The figure anticipated by the title is realized within the body of the poem in the description of the relation between the self and the God desired and desiring, which is expressed in terms of a compass image:

> Tú vienes con mi norte hacia mi sur,
> tú vienes de mi este hasta mi oeste. . .

> *You come with my north and toward my south,*
> *you come from my east up to my west. . .*

But the closing lines of the stanza affirm that the self's center is also the center of God, for God *is* the *centro rayeante,* and the image must therefore be regarded both as one of movement outward from the self, in an overflowing of creativity and love like the emanationism of the Neoplatonists, and as an inward movement of contemplation, responding love, and the sense of dependent relatedness.[26]

Looking back upon the trajectory of the circle in the poetry of Jiménez, we see that it shows a development of meaning increasingly positive and profound. In the earliest years it sometimes suggests an effort—only partly successful or basically unsuccessful—to capture the beauty of a passing moment, but at other times it evokes a sense of confinement in an oppressively limited world.

---

[26] It must, nevertheless, be pointed out that the starlike image of the *centro rayeante* is anticipated in some lines in *Poesía* in which a similar figure represents the poetic work: "—En un punto, chispa inmensa/ y breve, de puntas libres/ y de redondez esclava." '—In one moment, spark immense/ and brief, with free points/ and enslaved circularity.' The example shows again how Jiménez's thought contained implicit structures which were constant in his work long before they received explicit expression.

After the beginning of the Second Period, in 1916, the circle becomes a symbol of spiritual self-sufficiency, as through a kind of *via negativa,* there occurs a rejection of everything that is not mind. Finally, the poet discovers the transcendent depth within the center, through which the inwardly directed self symbolically finds a new relation to the outside world in its totality, and to this transcendent depth the poet gives the name *dios.*

It is, of course, clear, from the very beginning of *Animal de fondo,* that this God is not at all that of Catholic orthodoxy. The first poem in the book says to this divinity,

> No eres mi redentor, ni eres mi ejemplo,
> ni mi padre, ni mi hijo, ni mi hermano;
> eres igual y uno, eres distinto y todo;
> eres dios de lo hermoso conseguido,
> conciencia mía de lo hermoso. (*LP* 1289)

> *You are not my redeemer, nor are you my example,*
> *nor my father, nor my son, nor brother;*
> *you are the same and one, you are distinct and all;*
> *you are the God of beauty achieved,*
> *my consciousness of beauty.*

And elsewhere he says that he has been "dudón en la leyenda/del dios de tantos decidores" (*LP* 1321), 'skeptic in the legend/ of the God of so many sayers,' making clear again his rejection of the religion of tradition, the religion which men teach and preach to one another. Even more important, however, are the "Notes" at the end of *Animal de fondo,* in which he declares that he has always found "in pantheistic mysticism the supreme form of beauty" and has always professed an "immanent religion without absolute creed." (*LP* 1341)

It is clear that in the final work these attitudes are still fully present, but brought to fruition in the concept of divinity "as a unique, just, universal consciousness of beauty which is both in us and outside us at the same time." (*LP* 1342) What is of critical importance in such a development is the concept of the universal consciousness as being both within and without, subject and object, immanent and transcendent. Some nine years before the experience of *Animal de fondo* he had said, "The best Spanish lyrics have been and are inevitably mystic, with God or without Him, since the poet . . . is a mystic without a necessary God."[27] Such a concept of mysticism is basically metaphysical, rather than religious, and as the poetry of that period clearly shows, the danger which it presents to the poet is that of a purely subjective immanentism. Therefore, although *Animal de fondo* contains no new 'doctrine,' the concept of consciousness as both subject and object and the appearance of a *Thou*-attitude toward objective consciousness permit—require—us to regard this as poetry of the mystic mode, basically analogous, as poetry, to that of the Christian mystical tradition, although clearly mediated and modified by the symbolist experience and the poet's inability to accept Catholic doctrine.[28]

It must, certainly, be granted that the distinction

[27] In the lecture, "Poesía y literatura." *El trabajo gustoso,* p. 41.
[28] See Oreste Macrì, "El segundo tiempo de la poesía de Jiménez," *La Torre,* II (1957), 287. Macrì rejects as absurd any attempt to relate Jiménez's poetic metaphysics to Spanish mysticism, insisting that its source is "el simbolismo franco–germánico." It is difficult, however, to see how one can ignore the analogies between metaphysics and the mystic mode of expression, even if one grants that in the crucial question of religious belief a profound gulf separates the two. It is equally difficult, in fact, to ignore Jiménez's frequently acknowledged debt to San Juan de la Cruz and his rather disputable but often repeated assertion that Spanish mysticism is the actual source of French symbolism.

between subjective and objective consciousness is not a sharp one, and as Professor Sánchez-Barbudo points out, it often disappears into complete ambiguity.[29] Such ambiguity is only natural if a mystic union has occurred between subject and object, but the very fact that the divinity is, in the first instance, not objective beauty but a 'universal consciousness of beauty' creates an intrinsic a priori ambiguity suggesting that the primary and fundamental phenomenon is one of subjectivity. This impression is strengthened also by the insistence, in the first two poems, that the experience described is one which is not revealed but "conseguido," 'achieved': "you are the God of beauty achieved" (*LP* 1289); "God. The achieved name of names." (*LP* 1292) Although 'achievement' might at times imply discovery, it also suggests creation, and at times it seems as though the God of this experience were being explicitly presented as the poet's own creation:

> El dios que es siempre al fin,
> el dios creado y recreado y recreado
> por gracia y sin esfuerzo. (*LP* 1292)

> *The God who ultimately always is,*
> *the God created, recreated and again created*
> *by grace and with no effort.*

In the "Notes," he avows that in his whole creative life he was "creating a world of which the goal was to be a God." (*LP* 1343)

Yet in spite of the reference to the 'God created,' it is not possible to interpret this as meaning merely that his God is an imagined divinity presiding over an imagined

[29] See his edition of *Dios deseado y deseante* (Madrid, 1964), p. 42 *et passim*.

world; it is true that He is contemplated within a world poetically created, but created through Him and for Him:

> Si yo, por ti, he creado un mundo para ti,
> dios, tú tenías seguro que venir a él,
> y tú has venido a él, a mí seguro,
> porque mi mundo todo era mi esperanza. (*LP* 1291)

> *If I, through You, created a world for You,*
> *God, You had to come in certainty to it,*
> *and You have come to it, to me in certainty,*
> *because my whole world was my hope.*

The concept of the divinity as both antecedent means and ultimate end of this creation tends, then, to reaffirm the objectivity of the universal consciousness which has been called God, and accords with the statement that it is both in us and outside us, itself both object of desire and subject of desiring. The fact that the objective consciousness has no attribute of personality beyond the second-person pronoun and, above all, the fact that it is 'achieved' rather than revealed are critical factors in establishing the conclusion that this is not at all Christian mysticism, but there can be no doubt of the poet's feeling that he has established a relationship of mutual love with an object external (though also internal) to himself, a universal object possessing a universal consciousness—that is, a world of both form and spirit.

There remains, of course, the question as to how successful the attempt to objectify consciousness has actually been. Can a universal object be considered truly an object, particularly if it is internal as well as external to the subject? For those ontological systems which insist that between subject and object there necessarily exists a layer of nothingness through which the subject knows the object as that which it itself is not,[30] the very affirmation of such an object fails if it seeks to be continuously and totally positive, and all that is actually affirmed is the plenitude of an impenetrable and opaque Being, wholly undifferentiated as to subject and object, or in any other way. It is, then, impenetrable precisely to the extent that it is affirmed, and therefore it becomes unavailable to consciousness. But if pure Being is thus hidden in darkness, it is for consciousness as if it were not—that is, consciousness itself is not—as is clearly implied in the proposition of Hegel which states that pure Being and pure Nothing are one and the same.[31] Similarly, in the philosophical thought of Antonio Machado, one sees that the circle, which for Parmenides was pure being, for Bonaventure Divine Being, and for Jiménez total being, is conceived of as the Great Zero or universal oval, that is, as nothingness, and the very fact that such a total reversal is possible is another indication of intrinsic paradox in the circle.[32]

Such, presumably, is the logic of a rationalistic ontology, but in Jiménez's poetic ontology the being which is wholly affirmed, far from quenching the negating

---

[30] I refer, of course, to the ontologies of Sartre and the Heidegger of "What is Metaphysics?"

[31] *The Science of Logic,* trans. William Wallace (Oxford, 1892), p. 161. It is appropriate to refer here also to an analogous concept expressed in Hegel's discussion of natural theology, since Jiménez's theology is precisely of this kind. Concerning the notion of God as the "abstract of positivity or reality, to the exclusion of all negation," he says, "It is with reason that the heart craves a concrete body of truth; but without definite feature, that is, without negation, contained in the notion, there can only be an abstraction. When the notion of God is apprehended only as that of the abstract or most real being, God is, as it were, relegated to another world beyond: and to speak of a knowledge of him would be meaningless. When there is no definite quality, knowledge is impossible. Mere light is mere darkness." *Logic,* p. 74.

[32] I refer to the sonnet, "Al gran cero," in Machado's *Cancionero apócrifo.*

discernment which is consciousness, is itself consciousness, yet still possessing a plenitude of being. Though reason may protest that such a synthesis of attributes is logically impossible,[33] the poet creates within a realm of pure freedom, wholly unfettered by the limitations of such reason and unconcerned about the question as to whether a verbal synthesis is radically different from a real one. His real concern is with a phenomenon which is basically an aspiration, not a limited and private one, but one of the oldest and most universal of human desires.

It is, then, because of his desire to attribute being to consciousness and consciousness to being that Jiménez uses the name which humanity has always regarded as embodying both attributes in the highest degree, and as realizing the synthesis to which it aspires: the name of God. And because the relation of the poet's self to this God is one of love, he is able to move outward, in love, to the reality of the surrounding world. Through the discovery of the 'God desired and desiring,' the world itself becomes desired and desiring, and the poet's relationship with it one of mutual desire and giving.

In the concluding lines of "Al centro rayeante," this final stage of the poet's spiritual trajectory is given its ultimate expression:

> Todo está dirijido
> a este tesoro palpitante,
> dios deseado y deseante,
> de mi mina en que espera mi diamante;
> a este rayeado movimiento
> de entraña abierta (en su alma) con el sol
> del día, que te va pasando en éstasis,
> a la noche, en el trueque más gustoso
> conocido, de amor y de infinito. (*LP* 1303)

---

[33] See Sartre, *Being and Nothingness*, pp. 89–90.

All things are directed
to this throbbing treasure,
God desired and desiring,
of the mine within which waits my diamond;
to this radiant movement
of opened heart (within the soul) by light
of day, which passes you in ecstasy,
to the night, in the exchange—most joyful ever known—
of love and of infinity.

V

The imperative to essentiality in poetry and in human desires seems, for Jiménez, to be grounded in an anguish which is, in the first instance, that of pain for the loss of beloved objects, for the passing of moments of joy and beauty into the darkness of the past. From this experience, there is projected into the future an anxious concern for the future states of being of all other beloved objects and of the subjective consciousness itself. Although the second anguish is, then, a derivative of the first one, it is no less deeply felt than the pain of experienced loss, and ultimately—in its subjective reference particularly—it constitutes the true existential anguish.

It is the first of these kinds of anguish which gives the strong note of melancholy and nostalgia to the whole of Jiménez's first poetic period. Such sentiments were, we know, partly the result of real tragedies—the death of the poet's father and that of his first love—and partly the product of the neurasthenic depression which required him to spend a number of years in his twenties and again in the last years of his life under psychiatric care. Partly, too, they were induced by the neo-romanticism of the symbolist movement with which Jiménez so thoroughly associated himself from the earliest years of his artistic maturity, but even in this case, to be sure, such sentiments were no mere pose, since they corresponded to a basic reality of his inner life.

It is principally as a quality of tone that the nostalgia is first manifested, and the autumnal park or garden is the constant symbol of grief for the death of beauty. Yet even when the vision is most strongly retrospective, there is a simultaneous awareness of the beauty which is still existent but tending toward nothingness:

> Y esa luz de ensueño y oro
> que muere en las hojas secas
> alumbra en mi corazón
> no sé qué vagas tristezas. (*PLP* 230, *Arias tristes*)

> *And that light of reverie and gold*
> *which is dying on the dry leaves*
> *enkindles within my heart*
> *I know not what vague sadnesses.*

From the image which combines a symbol of beauty already dead with one of present beauty fading into darkness there arises a sadness which is vague because it is total, for consciousness realizes that experience has revealed to it a universal law of existence.

At times the melancholy is expressed as specifically related to the dead beloved or to a lost joy, and sorrow for the loss is compounded by a willful rejection of resignation, and by the nurturing of the impossible hope for the restoration of a beauty which is irrevocably past:

> ¡Ay, quién pudiera
> componer una rosa deshojada;
> ver, de nuevo, en la aurora verdadera,
> la realidad de la ilusión soñada! (*PLP* 1296, *Laberinto*)

> *Oh, if I could*
> *compose the rose stripped bare,*
> *and see, again, in the dawn of truth,*
> *the reality of the dream, the aspiration!*

If the beauty is a present experience rather than of the past, desire seeks prolongation rather than return. If no less impossible than the wish to restore the beauty which is already lost, it is felt, perhaps, to be less inherently futile, and the eternally present ecstasy to which it aspires is the very time of the lyric itself. The experience of eternity in such a moment gives solace for temporal anxiety, but expression of the desire to prolong the experience is itself a sign of the return of that anxiety to consciousness:

> Lo eterno, en mí, está abierto como un tibio tesoro
> y, sobre la amargura del miedo cotidiano,
> llueve sus claridades de azul, de rosa, de oro. . .
>
> ¡Ay, prolongar eternamente esta dulce tarde,
> o morir ya, entre estas iluminadas flores! (PLP 867,
> *Elegías*)

> *The eternal, in me, is open like a warm treasure*
> *and, upon the bitterness of my daily fear,*
> *rains brightnesses of blue, of rose, of gold. . .*
>
> *Oh, to prolong eternally this gentle evening hour,*
> *or to die now, among the illumined flowers!*

The anguished uncertainty concerning future states of being is not only felt with respect to entities already known but is directed also toward those which have not yet begun to be. We have seen this in some lines quoted in Chapter III:

> ¡Oh, qué duda, qué afán, qué insomnio. . . ,
> este no saber nada de las rosas
> de la futura primavera! (*TA* 359)[1]

To regard the future with the melancholy of nostalgia is the same as regarding it as already past, and the poet explicitly recognized this in some lines written

---

[1] For the translation of these lines, see chap. III.   *159*

toward the end of the first period, precisely when melancholy was strongest:

> Y nuestro corazón, dejado y visionario,
> se anega, largamente, en un llanto romántico
> como si el porvenir hubiese ya pasado. . . (*PLP* 1408)

> *And our heart, abandoned and visionary,*
> *is slowly overcome in a romantic weeping,*
> *as if the future were already past.*

In such a view of the future there is a certain external resemblance to some aspects of a Christian *contemptus mundi,* as expressed, for example, in the *Coplas* of Jorge Manrique in the fifteenth century:

> Pues si vemos lo presente
> cómo en un punto se es ido
> y acabado,
> si juzgamos sabiamente,
> daremos lo no venido
> por passado.

> *For if we see how the present*
> *in a moment is ended*
> *and gone,*
> *if we judge wisely,*
> *we will regard what has not come*
> *as already past.*

But it is clear that an attitude which, in the fifteenth century, was the wisdom of Christian stoicism is in the young Jiménez a spiritual sickness, like that which Don Pablo in Azorín's *Doña Inés* calls the *mal de Hoffman,* the ultimate development of an all-consuming romantic nostalgia, which considers the future fully as lost as the past.

Ultimately, to be sure, this anxiety concerning the

future being of all objects of experience is grounded in the anguish of the conscious self for its own future being. It is known that the thought of death was Jiménez's chief obsession during his periods of depression, and death as a problem of human existence is clearly a principal theme of his poetry, if not, ultimately, the one major theme. Considering, though, how astonishingly prolific he was in the creation of his *obra poética,* and how important the theme of death is within it, it is almost surprising that the self-reference in his treatment of the theme is not more pronounced. One assumes that the very force of his anxiety made it possible for him only very rarely to take the prospect of his own death as an explicit theme of poetry, and this only when he had achieved the relative serenity of viewing it with poignant melancholy rather than with anxiety. One of the most effective of these is "El viaje definitivo," from the period 1910–11:

> . . .Y yo me iré. Y se quedarán los pájaros
> cantando;
> y se quedará mi huerto, con su verde árbol,
> y con su pozo blanco.
>
> Todas las tardes, el cielo será azul y plácido;
> y tocarán, como esta tarde están tocando,
> las campanas del campanario.
>
> Se morirán aquellos que me amaron;
> y el pueblo se hará nuevo cada año;
> y en el rincón aquel de mi huerto florido y encalado,
> mi espíritu errará, nostáljico. . .
>
> Y yo me iré; y estaré solo, sin hogar, sin árbol
> verde, sin pozo blanco,
> sin cielo azul y plácido. . .
> Y se quedarán los pájaros cantando. (*TA* 212)   *161*

*. . .And I shall go. And the birds will stay here
singing;
there will remain my garden, with its green tree,
and with its white well.*
    *Each afternoon, the sky will be placid and blue;
and there will ring, as they are ringing now,
the bells in the tower.*
    *And those who once loved me will die;
the village will be new each year;
and in that corner of my garden with flowers and white
    walls,
my spirit will wander, nostalgically. . .*
    *And I shall go; and be alone, with no hearth, or green
tree, with no white well,
no blue and placid sky. . .
And the birds will stay here singing.*

The period in which the poem was written came at
the end of a decade of recurring severe depressions, and
just prior to a return to a very active life in Madrid in
which he would direct the publications of the *Residen-
cia de Estudiantes* and begin his courtship of Zenobia
Camprubí. Despite the strongly elegiac tone expressed
principally, perhaps, by the insistent assonantal rhyme
in *á-o* which sounds a continuous lament through the
entire poem, it must be said that the evitable and definitive separation of the subjective consciousness from all
familiar and beloved objects of its experience is here
contemplated with an eye undimmed by a single tear.
Pathos and sentiment are very evidently present, but
both are fully controlled and subordinated to the value
of resignation to the simple but catastrophic fact of the
definitive separation which is death, as expressed in the
contrast between " . . .Y yo me iré" and "Y se quedarán."

Probably much less serene was the moment in which
Jiménez revised the poem for inclusion in the anthology, *Canción,* in which the "estaré solo" is replaced by

"seré otro," 'I shall be another.' It is evident from the change that the poet came to regard the subjective consciousness as being so defined by the objects of its experience that when separated from them it is separated from itself—no longer *is* itself. It is, in fact, this realization which seems to the poet in the second version to be the greatest tragedy in death.

The extreme of pessimism occurring in the poems of *Melancolía,* which date from the same period as the previous poem, is overcome in all subsequent works (but not in the emotional life of the poet himself), and if notes of anxiety and melancholy continue to be heard in them, it is clear that Jiménez is also able to achieve in them some degree of serenity and resignation in the face of the painful realities of temporal existence.

This he does by 'intellectual' means, which are not, of course, those of discursive reason but of poetic intuition, through which he seeks to elaborate a new conception of life and death and of time itself, which will convince him that sorrow for the past and anxiety for the future is groundless. Particularly frequent in *Eternidades* (1916–17) and *Piedra y cielo* (1917–18) is the concept that the loss and forgetting of the past is not to be regretted but eagerly to be sought. The contrast with the naïve nostalgia of the first period could not be greater:

> No busques, alma, en el montón de ayer,
> más perlas en la escoria.
> La primavera del futuro
> es toda de hojas nuevas para ti. (*LP* 679, *Eternidades*)

> *Soul, do not seek in the heap of yesterday*
> *for more pearls in the dross.*
> *The springtime of the future*
> *is all of new leaves for you.*

163

Eventually, in fact, there comes the realization that even if he could stop the passing of time, he would himself immediately move away from that kind of static eternity. With great self-irony, he writes a brief poem entitled "Nostaljia," which is an incisive criticism of his own spiritual restlessness:

> ¡Este ansia de apurar
> todo lo que se va;
> de hacerlo permanente,
> para irme de su siempre! *(LP 964, Poesía)*

> *This anxiety to drain the fullness*
> *from everything that passes;*
> *and to make it permanent,*
> *only to depart, myself, from its 'forever.'*

The ideal, then, is that of liberation from the burden of the past, which will enable the spirit to live more fully the present and future:

> ¡Oh tiempo, dame tu secreto,
> que te hace más nuevo cuanto
> más envejeces!
> Día tras día, tu pasado
> es menor, y tu porvenir más grande,
> —y tu presente
> ¡lo mismo siempre que el istante
> de la flor del almendro!—
> ¡Tiempo sin huellas:
> dame el secreto con que invade,
> cada día, tu espíritu a tu cuerpo!
> *(LP 564, Eternidades)*

> *Oh time, give me your secret,*
> *which makes you newer, the more*
> *you grow old!*
> *Day after day your past*
> *is less, and your future greater,*
> *—and your present*
> *the same always as the instant*
> *of the flower of the almond!—*

Time without footprints:
give me the secret whereby,
each day, your spirit invades your body!

Like the 'roses without history' in one of the poems discussed in Chapter III, the flower of the almond is the symbol of a present moment completely unfettered by any tie with the past, having a duration which is virtually limited to an instant of the present and yet is eternal. Contained within it, then, is a view of the present based on the paradox of the eternal moment.

At one point in *Piedra y cielo,* there occurs a real exaltation of the liberation which occurs through forgetting, but with an emphasis different from that of the previous poem:

¡Olvido, hermoso olvido,
libertador final
de nuestro nombre puro
en la imajinación del tiempo feo!
    —Hombres, hombres, hombres. . . , ¡ay!
¡Oh, venideros días,
en que el alma, olvidada con su nombre
habrá estado, en si, en todo,
y no estará, con otro, en nada! (*LP* 823)

Forgetting, fair forgetting,
the final liberator
of our pure name
in the imagination of foul time!
    Oh, men, men, men!
    Oh, future days,
in which the soul, forgotten with its name
will in itself have been in everything,
and will not with another be in anything!

This desire for forgetting is, of course, actually a desire to be forgotten by others, and Jiménez's chief concern in these lines is with that self which his own renown has caused to be held captive, not so much by the past as by the minds of other men. It is, then, a kind of being for others which he seeks to free and to have returned to his own intimate consciousness. The prospect of a future time in which that intimate self and its fame will be forgotten is eagerly contemplated, and it is clear that if death is the price of such freedom, it will not be considered too high.

The consolation for death is in the thought of the time when the soul 'will in itself have been' in everything, that is, as a free contemplating subject, unhampered by the notice of other men, and 'will not with another be' in anything, will not be the captive of other consciousness through any kind of co-presence. The feeling that being with another inevitably leads to such captivity makes, of course, impossible any feeling of plural subjectivity and leads to the ultimate solipsism.[2]

What is known of Jiménez's life shows clearly that the desire to abolish the past as past for the sake of an eternal present is implicit in his attitude toward the whole of his poetic work, as well as being expressed in individual poems. Intimately related to this rejection of the past and the exaltation of forgetfulness is his rejection of virtually the whole of his work before the *Diario*, at least in the original versions, which made him ruthlessly destroy every copy he could find of his early first editions.[3] Only when a poem had been *revivido*—

[2] This captivity is the same as that which Sartre calls "the solidification and alienation of my own possibilities," which is effected by the look of the Other. (*Being and Nothingness,* p. 263.) The co-presence which Jiménez here rejects is clearly not a true plural subjectivity but precisely those objectlike others who themselves make an object of his subjectivity or—more accurately—superimpose a being for others upon his being for itself.

[3] Juan Guerrero Ruíz recounts an incident in which he told Jiménez of having found a copy of *Rimas,* the poet's third book, published in 1902. At the same time he told him quite frankly

'relived'—was it accepted as part of the living present and included in an anthology, and it is clear that to speak of 'reliving' for 'revising' was not merely a capricious metaphor. For although at times the 'relived' versions are undoubtedly superior to the originals—as the poem quoted at the beginning of Chapter II clearly shows—it is often obvious that changes have been made for their own sake, simply because of the need to give a poem a form which is of a new present.

A form of consolation for death quite different from that in the previous poem was achieved in one written for the unpublished collection entitled *La muerte,* dated 1919–20, and therefore subsequent to the period of *Piedra y cielo*. The annihilation of the past, of 'what has been,' is no longer acceptable, but anxiety is now overcome by the consideration that 'what has been' has a perpetual reality of which we can always—in some sense—say that 'it is':

> No es la vida quien tiene que temer
> a la muerte, sino la muerte.
> El vivir que ha pasado, no ha pasado,
> como no pasa el día en que nacimos,
> ni el sueño que soñamos, ni la rosa
> que olimos, ni el abrazo
> que nos dieron, ni el libro que leímos.
> No está muerto el pasado,
> y la ruina vive,
> y muertos viviremos muertos,
> **si vivimos**
> mientras viva la vida.

---

that he had no intention of letting him see it, since he knew his mania for destroying copies of his early works. However, after Jiménez had insisted that he needed a copy of it for the preparation of his *Obras completas* and after repeated promises that he would return the book unharmed, his friend agreed to let him have it, only to have to record in a footnote: "I left it for him and he tore it up." See Juan Guerrero Ruíz, *Juan Ramón de viva voz* (Madrid, 1961), p. 159.

No es nuestra vida la que muere,
porque no muere lo que ha sido.
Lo que muere es la muerte.[4]

It is not life that must fear
death, but rather death.
Living that has passed has not all passed,
as does not pass the day when we were born,
nor the dream we have dreamed, nor the rose
that we savored, nor the book we read.
The past is not dead,
the ruin lives,
and, dead, we shall live in death,
if we live
as long as life shall live.
It is not our life that dies,
for what has been does not die.
That which dies is death.

These verses are not, certainly, as successful in lyricizing the theme as most of Jiménez's other poems on death, but their importance lies in their explicit presentation of an attitude toward the passing of time which made it possible for him to achieve—in certain moments, at least—the serenity of resignation to the inevitability of death. In the achievement of such serenity lies, in fact, the poet's only hope for life in death. For the affirmation that 'dead, we shall live in death,' is not one of belief in a future life as such, but is based upon a concept of the unity of temporal reality according to which 'what has been' is fully as real as 'that which is.' It therefore becomes important to live fully in the present, excluding from it any of that anticipated experience of death which is anxiety, in order that the eternity of

[4] The manuscript of this poem is in the possession of Sr. Don Francisco Hernández-Pinzón Jiménez, to whom I am indebted for a copy of the text. It will be included in a forthcoming volume of *Libros inéditos de poesía*.

what has been may contain as much of life and as little of death as possible.

By means of such concepts, then, Jiménez tries to free himself from the kind of existential concern with death which Unamuno considered the essence of wisdom and which Juan Ramón himself had suffered so profoundly —at times pathologically. But it is clear that he was never able to free himself definitively from the thought of death, and at times, in fact, he seems to have concluded that the acceptance of that thought and of the loss through forgetting of past moments of existence brings about a spiritual renewal which is itself like a new birth:

> Al abrir hoy los ojos
> a la luz, he pensado
> —por vez primera—
> con gusto—¡corazón mío!—en la muerte.
>   Ha sido igual que otro
> nacer, como un entrenacer,
> entre el nacer primero
> y el último, el morir.
>   Y los recuerdos
> de mi vida de antes, se han quemado
> en el sol grande del olvido. (*LP* 817, *Piedra y cielo*)

> *Today, when opening my eyes*
> *to light, I thought*
> *—for the first time—*
> *with pleasure—oh, my heart—of death.*
>   *It was just like another*
> *birth, an internascence,*
> *between a first birth*
> *and the last, which is death.*
>   *And memories*
> *of all my former life were burned*
> *in the great sun of forgetting.*

In earlier poems concerning his own death, Jiménez's thought was fixed in contemplation of the time when he would no longer exist, but here the 'running forward in thought' to that time is seen to have positive consequences for the present and for the whole of life.[5] The 'pleasure' which he experiences in this thought is not the result of any unbearable anguish or disappointments with the things of this life, but is due simply to the fact that a profoundly felt awareness of life's end at some unknown point in the future gives it a 'horizon,' a form of limitation which, as we said of the horizons in the innumerable sunsets of the poet's first period, is the basic requirement of form. It becomes possible, therefore, to view the whole of what remains of life as a trajectory, a movement through time which has a specific form as well as direction. Thereby, life acquires a new and intrinsic purpose and meaning, for here too, form does not merely *have* a meaning, it *is* a meaning. In later years, Jiménez gave to the form of human life the name *destino* (referring not only to that which is future but also to what is of the past), of which more will be said at a later point.

So profound is the sense of a new birth or of having begun for the first time really to live which the acceptance of death is able to give, that the whole of life prior to the moment of acceptance can now really be forgotten gladly, for life before that moment was devoid of direction and form. The reference in the second quatrain to death as a 'last birth' seems, of course, to be an attempt to find consolation in the hope of an after-life,

[5] The anticipation of death here referred to as a 'running forward in thought' is suggested by the Heideggerian concept of *Vorlaufen,* the anticipation of death which "turns out to be the possibility of understanding one's *ownmost* and uttermost potentiality-for-Being—that is to say, the possibility of *authentic existence.*" I quote Martin Heidegger, *Being and Time,* trans. John Macquarrie and Edward Robinson (London, 1962), p. 307.

and it certainly could not be asserted that the words in any way reject such a hope. But their principal intent is probably just to emphasize the analogy between birth and death—and possibly also the 'inter-birth' of which the poet speaks—as terminal points of transition whose chief significance is their function in giving form to the time of human life. If it assumes a new form beyond the moment of death the poet's vision cannot discover. Death, however, like forgetting, or like any absolute break with the past, is necessary for a further beginning to be really new, and therefore the poem will say that death is birth, just as one of Jiménez's aphorisms says, "To forget is to come alive."[6]

But there are still moments—probably more characteristic ones—when the desire is not to 'burn memories' but to preserve them, and it is usually accompanied by an anxiety caused by the evanescence of the remembered experience or image:

> ¡No te vayas, recuerdo, no te vayas!
> ¡Rostro, no te deshagas así,
> como la muerte!
> ¡Seguid mirándome, ojos grandes, fijos,
> como un momento me mirasteis! (*LP* 705)

> *Do not go, memory, do not go!*
> *Image, do not fade away like that,*
> *like death!*
> *Continue looking at me, eyes, so large and steady,*
> *as once you looked at me.*[7]

---

[6] *La colina de los chopos*, p. 146. Jiménez's concept of life as a constant passing through death to newness of being is commented upon extensively in Basilio de Pablos, *El tiempo en la poesía de Juan Ramón Jiménez*.

[7] Cf. the sonnet, "¿Cómo era, Dios mío, cómo era?" (*LP* 26) which will be commented upon in chap. VI.

These lines occur in *Piedra y cielo* as part of the same series on memory in which we found the lines commented upon in Chapter I as expressing the concept of memory as essence, that is, as eternity ("Istante, sigue, sé recuerdo . . . ¡Oh, sí, pasar, pasar, no ser istante,/ sino perenidad en el recuerdo!"), and there may at first appear to be a certain contradiction between the expression in one poem of the desire for the present instant to pass and, in another, for memory not to slip away. It is clear, though, that both poems accept and express the movement of time and both are concerned with memory as a means of finding stability within time's flow. The real difference is that the earlier poem ("Istante, sigue") assumes that the stability is secure and is anxious only for the present to pass in order that its experience may enter the eternity of memory, while the later one expresses the anxiety that memory too may be borne away in the flow of time. In both cases, one feels clearly the inner rhythm of that flow, which is the dynamism of time itself.

This dynamism has been referred to earlier as "successiveness"—*sucesión* is Jiménez's term—a phenomenon which is the primary empirical quality of time itself and one which assumes a major importance in the poetry and critical thought of the poet's second period. In the lecture, "La razón heroica," for example, he insists that

the poet is internal and external successiveness, through given time and space. And he who conceives eternity or time as ancient is one who has no consciousness of his own time or of his own possible eternity; one who can not conceive of his immanence, one who does not realize or care about his own destiny. A poet who is only traditional in spirit or form, one who is a poet only with respect to the past, might be a good one and please himself, but he will not fulfill his luminous function, he will not pass on his torch from day to day, within himself or for others. The myth of the return, of the eternal youth and spring, is that of poetry itself. (*TG* 118–19)

The reference to the myth of the eternal return is of special interest to us in so far as it constitutes another manifestation of the infinite circle in Jiménez's thought. Although his discussion of *sucesión* may seem at first to suggest only linear temporality stretching on indefinitely, it seems that any attempt to represent conceptually the whole of successiveness almost necessarily assumes the form of the circle, as it had in the thought of St. Bonaventure. The reference to the myth at the end of the paragraph quoted above is not logically anticipated, but it naturally develops from the idea of eternal successiveness.

At the same time, *Piedra y cielo* shows a development of the concept of the 'eternal instant' in the direction of what might be called a 'present of simultaneity,' a present which does not merely include the past as past— which is the best that memory can do in ordinary human experience—but renders it actually present, simultaneous with what we ordinarily call present and with the future as well.[8] The nearest approach to such an ideal in the natural realm is found in art, and this is emphatically asserted to be the goal of the poet's work:

> ¡Quisiera que mi libro
> fuese, como es el cielo por la noche,
> todo verdad presente, sin historia!

[8] What is here called a 'simultaneous present' is, therefore, an eternal present, which Poulet shows to have long been the usual concept of eternity itself: in Parmenides a *homou pan,* in Boethius a *totum simul,* in Scotus Eriugena a *contractio totius temporis praesentialiter habita in conspectu omnia videntis.* (See Poulet, pp. iv–v and xxv.)

> Que, como él, se diera en cada istante,
> todo, con sus estrellas; sin
> que niñez, juventud, vejez quitaran
> ni pusieran encanto a su hermosura inmensa.
>   ¡Temblor, relumbre, música
> presentes y totales!
> ¡Temblor, relumbre, música en la frente
> —cielo del corazón—del libro puro! (*LP* 828)

> *I would wish my book to*
> *to be, as is the heaven at night,*
> *all present truth, with no past history.*
>   *That like it, it might give itself, at each instant,*
> *completely, with all its stars; without*
> *childhood, youth, or old age taking from*
> *or adding to the charm of its immense beauty.*
>   *Trembling, light, music,*
> *present and total!*
> *Trembling, light, music in the face*
> *—heaven of the heart—of the pure book!*

This is not only an ideal for art, however; for the poet whose life is subsumed in art, the aesthetic ideal is also an ideal of life. At another point in *Piedra y cielo,* Jiménez exclaims, "¡Hagamos grande sólo la verdad presente!" 'Let us make large only the present truth!' But to say that the simultaneous present is an ideal is, in effect, to say that it is an essential truth of temporal reality, not an empirical one. In the simultaneous present are included a vision of what is and of what has been, both as essential realities permanently projected into the future. Such a present contains successiveness because the order of being found within it does itself contain it and makes it permanent.

The simultaneous present is, then, no mere static vision; it, too, is a manifestation of the *éstasis dinámico.* Inevitably, however, its effect is to emphasize ecstasy rather than dynamism, so that although successiveness is implicit within it, it is not strikingly felt. There are moments moreover, when Juan Ramón realizes that memory and the thirst for the future are not merely in contrast but in conflict, and that to give adequate and equal expression to both of them is the principal problem of his poetry. A number of the aphorisms of the same period attempt to express this ambivalence:

> *My idea would be to forget and act.*
> *And I remember, remember, remember, and do not act.*
>
> *If only, time, I could hurry you and stop you at the same time.*
>
> *The ideal is that of a present which would be like a mean between an infinite flight forward, held back infinitely from behind.*[9]

The last of these doubtless succeeds most fully in expressing the balance between the two desires, but an even more effective expression of it is in a brief aphoristic poem from *Belleza* which has the title, "La corriente infinita," one which he used more than once because it expressed so well his sense of time:

> Mi alma corre, agua pura,
> entre una orilla de oro de recuerdo
> y otra dorada de esperanza,
> reflejando en un punto ambas pasiones
> y haciéndolas iguales, en su fuga
> hacia la eterna novedad. (*LP* 1076)
>
> *My soul runs, a pure water,*
> *between one golden shore of memory*
> *and another golden shore of hope,*
> *reflecting in the same instant both passions*
> *and making them equal, in its flight*
> *toward the eternal newness.*

[9] *La colina de los chopos*, pp. 198 and 202.

Such a precise equilibrium is not often so well achieved, but it becomes the norm of the later poetry in the second period, and Jiménez explores every possibility for overcoming the sense of tension and conflict between memory and the desire for newness. Beyond equilibrium he seeks to achieve a real synthesis of all of time. There is, in *La estación total,* a triptych of poems entitled "Paraíso," in the first section of which eternity is described as "lo que sigue," which must mean not so much 'what comes after' as 'what continues to be what it has been,' for the phrase is followed by the appositive, "lo igual," 'what is the same.' We must examine this section as a whole:

Como en la noche, el aire ve su fuente
oculta. Está la tarde limpia como
la eternidad.
          La eternidad es sólo
lo que sigue, lo igual; y comunica
por armonía y luz con lo terreno.
    Entramos y salimos sonriendo,
llenos los ojos de totalidad,
de la tarde a la eternidad, alegres
de lo uno y lo otro. Y de seguir,
y de entrar y de seguir.
                      Y de salir. . .
(Y en la frontera de las dos verdades,
esaltando su última verdad,
el chopo de oro contra el pino verde,
síntesis del destino fiel, nos dice
qué bello al ir a ser es haber sido.)   (*LP* 1138)

As in the night, the air sees its fountain
hidden. The afternoon is pure as
eternity.
      Eternity is only
what continues, that which is the same; communing
by harmony and light with earthly things.   *176*

We enter and go out smiling,
our eyes filled with totality,
from afternoon to that which is eternal, glad
in one and the other. And to continue,
to enter and continue.
                                        And to go out. . .
(And on the frontier of the two realities,
exalting the ultimate reality,
the poplar of gold against the green pine,
synthesis of faithful destiny, tells us
how fair when going to be is to have been.)

The hatred for the past which was the reaction of
Juan Ramón's middle years against the naïve nostalgia
of his early poetry, is now overcome, and the conflict
between memory and forgetting, between past and future, is resolved: 'How fair when going to be is to have
been.' The essential beauty of the poplar of gold against
the green pine teaches us to accept the continuing presence of the past as, in the present, we look toward the
future. All three of these modes or ecstasies of temporality are eternal because they are changeless realities
which together form the single reality of the simultaneous present, the eternity whose truth is complementary to that of the empirical reality of change and
joined to it by the existent beauty itself, that of the
poplar and the pine.[10] The 'two realities' of the afternoon and eternity, between which the consciousness joy-
fully moves in free alternation, are, to be sure, distinct
realms of being, separated by a definite frontier, but the
ultimate beauty is that of their basic unity. Yet the final
line shows clearly that what was first presented as a
contrast between the afternoon—the empirical experi-

---

[10] A prose poem from the late twenties describes such a moment
as an 'Ecstasy of the moment, existent *and therefore* eternal'
(italics mine). *La colina de los chopos*, p. 189.

ence of time in a particular present—and eternity is the same as the contrast between 'going to be' and 'having been.' Therefore the empirical present is the moment of 'going to be,' while eternity is 'what has been.'[11]

The image of the poplar against the pine, described as a 'synthesis of faithful destiny,' must, then, symbolize the combination of past and present/future which constitutes the whole of temporal reality. Although there is nothing that explicitly reveals to which of the realities each tree corresponds, it can scarcely be doubted that the poplar, with a treasure of accumulated time in the gold of its leaves, represents the eternity of 'having been,' while the pine is the moment of 'going to be,' ever verdant but also darkly mysterious and partly hidden by the brilliance of beauty already achieved. The concept of 'destiny,' as we shall observe in other occurrences of the term, refers to that structure of time which results from the synthesis of the two realities, the adjective 'faithful' being one which will acquire a particular significance in the poems of the final years in expressing concepts of coherence and continuity.

Inevitably, to be sure, the synthesis of eternity and time presents the appearance of an assimilation of time to eternity, but it is never a purely static one. Whenever he tended toward such a view of temporal reality, Jiménez always reacted immediately against it, as the second section of the triptych clearly shows:

> Hondo vaivén de sólidos y luces
> traslada la estación de un sitio a otro.

[11] Jiménez so often returns to the idea that what has been is eternal, it is only natural that one definition of eternity should prove to be 'that which has been.' Cf. the Hegelian concept of essence as 'what has been' which we have previously seen implied in other poems of Jiménez.

Enmedio del viraje natural
¡qué hacer con nuestra loca vida abierta!
　　Ya no sirve esta voz ni esta mirada.
No nos basta esta forma. Hay que salir
y ser en otro ser el otro ser.
Perpetuar nuestra esplosión gozosa. (*LP* 1139)

> *Deep ferment of solids and of lights*
> *transports the season from place to place.*
> *Within the natural gyration,*
> *what shall be done with our wild, open life!*
> *This voice no longer serves, nor this way of looking.*
> *This form will not suffice. One must go forth*
> *and be in other being the other being.*
> *Perpetuate the joyful explosion.*

Thus, the ideal is still that of dynamism, successive-ness, and the perpetual transcendence of self and of every achieved moment of time, even in the form of an explosively centrifugal flight from every established center of being. The opening lines of the second of these stanzas are also a call for constant renewal of poetic language, but more important than their reference to the activity of writing is their significance with respect to human reality itself, implying both the acceptance of the inevitable fact of successiveness in the life of man, and the desirability of finding a new vision and a new voice to express it in each successive moment.[12]

The last section of the triptych, entitled "El oto-ñado," is basically retrospective, doubtless in recogni-tion of the fact that in the autumn of his years the poet's sum of lived experience constitutes a much larger por-

---

[12] Awareness of the need for a constant renewal of poetic language is, of course, itself a primary characteristic of modern poets and a frequent theme in their work. Cf. the lines—strikingly similar to those of Jiménez—in T. S. Eliot's *Little Gidding:* "For last year's words belong to last year's language/ And next year's words await another voice."

tion of his total destiny than does that which lies before him. Instead of looking upon the past as something irretrievably lost, however, he regards it as an accumulated treasure which in the autumn of life he has seen come to full maturity and made so fully his own that its totality is identified with him:

> Estoy completo de naturaleza,
> en plena tarde de áurea madurez,
> alto viento en lo verde traspasado.
> Rico fruto recóndito, contengo
> lo grande elemental en mí (la tierra,
> el fuego, el agua, el aire) el infinito.
> Soy tesoro supremo, desasido,
> con densa redondez de limpio iris,
> del seno de la acción. Y lo soy todo.
> Lo todo que es el colmo de la nada,
> el todo que se basta y que es servido
> de lo que todavía es ambición. (*LP* 1140)

> *I am complete now with the whole of nature,*
> *in a mid afternoon gold and mature,*
> *lofty wind in the penetrated green.*
> *Rich, hidden fruit, I contain*
> *what is great and elemental (earth,*
> *fire, water, air) the infinite.*
> *I am the supreme treasure, disengaged,*
> *by dense encircling of limpid iris,*
> *from the breast of the action. I am all,*
> *the all which is the fullness of the nothing,*
> *the all which is sufficient and is master*
> *of what remains in me of future hope.*

The final vision within the series is, then, that of a life brought to a fullness of maturity which makes the entire world its own. The longing for pantheistic union with nature—so urgent in Juan Ramón's early years—has been accomplished, not through a dissolution of the self, but by appropriating the cosmos to the self, giving the subjective consciousness of the world the structure of a 'dense encircling.' The world has become the poet's own through his experience of it, and since that experience is a permanent one, its object, the world, is an equally permanent possession.

It is as though the poet's intuition corroborated the validity of the Spanish idiom which expresses a person's age by saying that he 'has' so many years, for Jiménez's view of the past is such that he can regard it with the serene assurance that the past years and all that they contain are something he really does 'have'; what remains to him of life and its hopes is complementary to this past, which already contains the greater part of the totality. In this way, then, he is able to conclude that the totality is 'master of what remains in (him) of future hope.'

Looking back upon his own life in his years of late maturity, Jiménez sees the past also as structured time, a trajectory not yet complete but already discernible in its ultimate form. To the concept of life as figured time, Juan Ramón gives the name *Destino,* the 'destiny' which appeared in the first poem of the triptych and is generally used in the poet's last years with a meaning which implies not only 'future fate' but also 'realized past.'[13] In the prose poem *Espacio,* he regards it as having a form so complete as to endow it with the eternal reality and self-sufficiency of divinity itself:

> I am my Destiny and no one and nothing more than I; therefore I believe in It and oppose nothing in It, in myself, for It is more than the usual gods, the other god, governed, like me by Destiny, distributer of substance with essence. In

[13] In Jiménez's last project for the definitive revision and ordering of his complete works, he planned to use the name *Destino* as the title for the whole collection, clearly revealing thereby his conception of it as an image of his own life if not, indeed, identical with it.

the beginning was Destiny, father of Action and grand-
father or great-grandfather—or something even more re-
mote—of the Word. I raise my anchor, therefore, so that It
may blow more easily with its wind over the serene or terrible, atlantic, mediterranean, pacific, or whatever they may
be. . . Any form is the form that Destiny, form of death
or life, form of taking and leaving, leaves or takes; and it is
useless to flee from it or to seek it. (*TA* 869)

If the destiny of the past is life formed 'as of the
present moment,' it is death which gives life its definitive form. In the very moving poem on the death of
Ruben Darìo, to whom Jiménez and his contemporaries
owed so much in the modernist renewal of Hispanic
poetry, this concept is already clearly suggested:

> Sí. Se le ha entrado
> a América su ruiseñor errante
> en el corazón plácido. ¡Silencio!
> Sí. Se le ha entrado
> a América en el pecho
> su propio corazón. Ahora la tiene,
> parado en firme, para siempre,
> en el definitivo
> cariño de la muerte. (*LP* 290–91, *Diario*)

> *Yes. To America he has returned,*
> *her wandering singer, entering*
> *her placid heart. Keep silent!*
> *Yes. To the bosom of America*
> *has now returned*
> *her own heart. Now she holds him,*
> *stopped quite still, forever,*
> *in the definitive*
> *affection of death.*

The poem is the first of an important series of
verses—scattered throughout the works of the Second
Period—in which the occasion of writing a poem to the
memory of a friend inspired Jiménez to a particularly
striking profundity of thought and beauty of expres-

sion. The emotion packed into the lines quoted above may be due as much to an anxious preoccupation with his own death as it is to the loss of his friend—a thought never wholly absent from even the most disinterested grief—but the direction of attention toward an analysis of the phenomenology of death gives that emotion a classic restraint which makes it a possible and strikingly effective material for poetic art. The concept of death as the ultimate possibility, which gives life its fixed and definitive form is the same as that expressed in the sentence of Malraux, quoted more than once by Sartre, according to which "the terrible thing about Death is that it transforms life into Destiny."[14] But the Destiny which for Malraux is a source of terror represents to Jiménez a triumph of form, that is, of art itself, and he accepts the term gladly as the name for both a life and a body of poetic work brought to definitive form.

The concept first suggested in the poem on the death of Darío is brought to a fuller development in the poems in *La estación total* dedicated to someone identified only as "La voluntaria M." In the fourth poem of the series, for example we find:

> ¡Qué plenitud, tú en lo definitivo,
> fundida a lo que nunca cambiará ya de historia;
> estensión de tu yedra, tu nueva vida solitaria
> por lo real profundo sin pasadiza forma;
> semilla verdadera de lo fijo, escultura, conciencia
> enquistada en la tierra que no se desmorona! (*LP* 1166)

> *What plenitude, you in what is definitive,*
> *united with what now will never change in history;*
> *extension of your vine, your new life in solitude*
> *in the profoundly real with no swiftly passing form;*

---

[14] For example, *Being and Nothingness*, p. 112.

many of the concepts explicit in it correspond very strikingly to a

true seed of what is fixed, sculpture, consciousness
encased in the realm which never decays!

The fact that in these lines it is the realm of death which is 'what is definitive' makes them externally similar to religious utterances which describe the afterlife as a stable paradise, free from all change and decay, but seen within the total context of Jiménez's thought they must be understood in a way which regards 'what is definitive' not as a place but as a mode of being of the person addressed. The plenitude of this definitive form of being is that of one that has achieved the impenetrable positivity of the past, the fullness of a being completely in itself.[15]

Similar to this, but adding to the concept of permanence and definitiveness a suggestion that transcendent intentionality (with inevitable temporal connotations) is itself a part of that permanence, is a poem included among the manuscripts of unpublished works now in the possession of Don Francisco Hernández-Pinzón Jiménez:

> Señor español de la belleza.
> Desde los montes de olas
> allí azules del Moncayo

[15] Here again Sartre's ontology proves extremely useful to us, since many of the concepts explicit in it correspond very strikingly to a number of Jiménez's intuitions concerning the ontological structure of consciousness. It is in the Sartrean sense, therefore, that reference is here made to 'in-itself' as that being "which is opaque to itself precisely because it is filled with itself" (*Being and Nothingness,* p. lxv) and possesses an identity of self with self succinctly expressed in the proposition that it "is what it is." (*ibid.*) What is spoken of in our text as the 'impenetrable positivity of the past' is, then, simply the opacity of being in-itself, for "the past is the ever-growing totality of the in-itself which we are" (p. 115), a totality terminated and made definitive at death.

nos ves venir a ti, maravillados,
y quieres que pasemos, que veamos
del otro lado tu gran rostro vuelto
igual en el azul y plata de las tres
que en el cárdeno y triste de las ocho.
   Igual en permanencia,
en superación
igual en hermosura nueva.

Spanish lord of beauty.
From the mountains of blue
waves there of Moncayo
you see us come to you, full of wonder,
and wish us to pass on and to see
from the far side your great face turned,
the same amid blue and silver at three
as in the sad scarlet at eight.
   The same in permanence,
in transcendent intention
the same in beauty always new.

The poem is untitled and bears no dedicatory note, but the reference to the Moncayo makes it seem clear that it is addressed to Antonio Machado, and every concept in it indicates that it was written after the death (in 1939) of Jiménez's great contemporary, whom in spite of long periods of estrangement he always profoundly admired. How deeply the latter's death affected him may perhaps be measured by the fact that he looks upon it almost as an invitation to pass on himself and look upon his friend's face from that other side, where it now remains forever the same, in spite of every shift in light and color as hour follows hour with the movement of the sun. But in terms of its implicit ontology, the way in which it most differs from the memorial to Darío is in the concept expressed in the last two lines, which sees an act of *superación* (translated as 'transcendent intention') and eternal newness (which implies renewal) of beauty as part of the definitive permanence of the dead.

But the clearest and at the same time the most beautifully moving expression of Jiménez's mature insight into the mode of being of the dead is found in the poem dedicated to the memory of Juan Ramón Jiménez Bayo, a nephew, who was killed fighting for the nationalist forces in the Spanish Civil War. With all its lyric simplicity, it is one of the great elegies of Spanish literature, and it must be quoted in full:

> Cantaron los gallos tristes
> como señal del destino;
> el hombre se puso en pie,
> miró sin sueño al abismo.
> Pero, ante la luz rojiza
> que recortó el roto pino,
> uno, que era diferente,
> siguió tendido lo mismo.
> Habló el otro que llegó,
> vino el animal sumiso,
> un humo olía a mujer,
> abrió la puerta el camino.
> El pájaro, el trigo, el agua,
> todo se erguía en lo limpio;
> pero no se levantaba
> uno, el que era distinto.
> (¿Dónde saludaba al pájaro,
> dónde oía el arroyillo,
> desde dónde se miraba,
> como otra espiga, tendido?)
> Pero no se levantaba
> uno, el que era distinto,
> pero no se levantó
> uno que estaba en su sitio.
> (Donde el que tendido está
> está de pie, como un río,
> sed una hecha agua una,
> solo leal espejismo.)
> Pero no se levantaba
> uno que ya estaba fijo,
> uno, el que estaba ya en él,
> uno, el fiel definitivo. (*TA* 905–06)

The sad cockerels sang out,
like a sign from destiny;
the man rose up and looked out
sleeplessly at the abyss.
    But, before the reddish light
outlining the broken pine,
one, different from the rest,
stayed there, lying as he was.
    Then another came and spoke,
the meek beast of burden came,
a smoke had the smell of woman,
the road opened wide the door.
    The bird, and the wheat, and water,
rose up in the dawn's pure air;
but he still did not rise up,
one distinct from all the rest.
    (Where was he greeting the bird,
where hearing the little brook,
where seeing himself, still lying,
and yet like a stalk of wheat?)
    But he still did not rise up,
one, distinct from all the rest,
never once did he arise,
one who was in his own place.
    (Where the one who lies there is,
he is standing, like a river,
single thirst made single water,
in one constant mirrored form.)
    But he still did not rise up,
one who was already fixed,
one, already in himself,
one, definitively true.

The analysis of the mode of being of the dead is made all the more meaningful in this poem by the contrast with that of the living, here represented by a family of peasants in the Andalucía where the young man had lived and where he died. Seldom, in fact, has any poet expressed so effectively the lonely 'differentness' of the dead, the poignancy of their separation from the life of labor and endeavor, from the companionship of wife and friends.

The crowing of the cocks at the start of a new day is the very symbol of temporality, marking the end of the night that has passed and calling all the living to continue filling out their destiny, which, even though it be as obscure as the abyss of darkness still surrounding the house, must be faced neither with fear nor illusion. They are comforted, to be sure, by the companionship of wives and friends, and even by the animals with which they live and work, but there is no tranquil stability in those relationships, for the demands of the road lying before them, the projects which provide the specific form of each individual destiny, are so imperative that the road itself opens the door and calls the man to be on his way. Such is the condition of those whose being is 'not yet' in itself and who stand—or rather, move—between being no longer what they have been and not yet what they will be. It is the condition of life and of consciousness, of being 'for itself,' at the heart of which is a void which it seeks constantly to fill with positive being.[16]

[16] The use here of the term 'being for itself' is, of course, also essentially Sartrean. It is the conscious and self-conscious being which in order to be conscious of itself must contain an internal negation, for consciousness is precisely an awareness in a subject that it is not its object. "The being of consciousness *qua* consciousness is to exist *at a distance from itself* as a presence to itself, and this empty distance which being carries in its being is Nothingness. Thus in order for a *self* to exist, it is necessary that the unity of this being include its own nothingness as the nihilation of identity." (p. 78.) In contrast to the in-itself, the proposition which most succinctly defines the for-itself describes it "as being what it is not and not being what it is." (p. lxv.) The single quotation marks used in the previous sentence are intended to make of the words 'not yet,' an oblique allusion to Heidegger's *Noch–nicht,* a basic character of Being of the human reality which he calls *Dasein.* The allusion is useful particularly because of a distinction Heidegger makes between the "not-yet" in the kinds of entities in which the passing of time brings with it a quantitative accrual of parts or units still out-

And in contrast to this is the condition of the 'different one,' to whom the poet's attention is turned in alternate glances in the first half of the poem, and who occupies it completely in the second half. Within the realm of the living he is different most obviously because he does not do what they do, having neither the verticality of the man who has awakened from sleep nor even that of the growing wheat. And this is the whole empirical truth concerning him.

The sequence of thought moves, then, from the level of the empirical—the observation of the 'differentness' of the dead one—to the level of the phenomenological, where that differentness is understood ontologically, as a contrast between the incomplete being of the living and the fullness of being in the dead. The 'different one' is in a place which is his own in the only absolute sense, fixed in the ultimate form which his life can take, and definitively true to it. The concept is precisely that of Mallarmé's *Tel qu'en Lui-même enfin l'éternité le change,* which Jiménez must certainly have known, and there may, indeed, be a distant echo of it in the penultimate line of the poem, which expresses the most significant difference between the living and the dead by saying very simply that the young man is 'in himself.' In terms of the ontological concepts implied within the poem, we may say that this means that his being is 'in

standing—that is, lacking—for the make-up of the total entity, of which the typical example would be the debt of money repaid over a period of time; and, on the other hand, the human entity called *Dasein,* of which the "not-yet" is an intrinsic character such that *Dasein* can never 'be' without it: "In Dasein there is undeniably a constant 'lack of totality' which finds an end with death. This 'not-yet' 'belongs' to Dasein as long as it is; this is how things stand phenomenally." (*Being and Time,* p. 286) ; "That Dasein should *be* together only when its "not-yet" has been filled up is so far from the case that it is precisely then that Dasein is no longer." (p. 287.)

itself,' in contrast to the being for itself of the living.[17]

The poet is never content, however, to accept as completely impenetrable the fullness of being in itself, and the empirical and phenomenological levels of vision are transcended in the parenthetical question and its answer, which attain to the poetic and mystical vision of a metaphysical reality. The question asks in what realm of reality the dead participate in acts of consciousness and self-consciousness—since they clearly do not do so in the empirical realm—and thereby it also asks the questions upon which it is implicitly based, the question as to whether any such realm exists and the one which asks if any form of human vision can penetrate it.

The implied longing to overcome the opacity of being in itself pertains not only to its external aspect, in the effort of the poet to project his own consciousness into it, but also to the internal aspect, that is, to the 'conscious' seeing, hearing, and speaking of one who is in himself and within being in itself. But for such consciousness to be possible, that being must contain finiteness, distinction of entities into subject and object, the void which separates being from being. In short, the fullness of being in itself must include the nothingness which makes consciousness possible.

The answer to the question 'where' is given only in terms of a 'how,' for the realm of the in-itself is not a place but a condition. The first thing said in the answer, then, is that the reality of being in itself is, as it

[17] As in-itself, it would, according to Sartre, be completely identical with itself and thereby lose all 'relatedness' to itself and to other beings, for identity is the null relation of self to self and of being to being. See Sartre, *Being and Nothingness*, p. 88. Cf. Heidegger's concept of death as the "ownmost nonrelational possibility," *Being and Time*, p. 294.

were, one of verticality with respect to the horizontal linearity of empirical time and space, for where the one who lies there is, he is not lying but standing, as only the living do in the state of the for-itself. Partly, to be sure, this may be understood in terms of the eternal reality of 'what has been,' and since verticality was once an intrinsic part of the man's human reality—part, that is, or his essence—it remains so eternally. But here we come to realize also that the whole of eternal reality intersects—perpendicularly, one might say—with empirical reality, and the dimensional otherness of eternity has its most effective symbol in the contrast between the two linearities, horizontal and vertical.

The play of paradox takes a new and surprising turn, however, when we read that the man is 'standing, like a river,' for with this, the contrast seems to break down completely, leaving us to conclude either that the horizontal dimension is the only real one or that we must accept the very strange image of a standing—that is, vertical—river. The fact is, however, that that image is one we have already seen in this poetry, presented in terms far too explicit to permit any doubt that it is, precisely, a vertical river which is intended:

> ¡Ay, cuándo, como en una
> fusión alta de estrella y de azucena,
> ascenderá mi chorro hasta encontrar
> —columna inalterable, río en pie—
> el chorro derramado de lo eterno! (LP, 854)

The lines were quoted in Chapter II as constituting a most significant phase in the development of the fountain symbol,[18] for the two jets of water symbolize the

---

[18] For the translation, see Chapter II.

longing of the self for the eternal and the response of eternity to that longing. There is a very notable quantitative difference, to be sure, between the thin jet of water symbolizing the self and its desire and the column or river of water that symbolizes the whole of eternity and the desire within it, but qualitatively they are but a single image. In the later poem we see that the vertical river may represent a man rather than the whole of eternity, which further confirms our belief that it is of the same essential meaning as the fountain image.

We therefore come to realize that the fountain represents transcendant aspiration not merely as one aspect of human reality, but as its very essence, seen under the species of eternity. This essential quality is one which has been referred to elsewhere as dynamism, temporality, and—most recently—as successiveness, and therefore we can now understand that these terms too are significant chiefly with respect to human reality. Indeed, in an essay quoted earlier in our discussion of the concept of successiveness, Jiménez in another passage tells us very specifically that that quality is intrinsic in man himself: "Society and man are only and always successiveness, provisionality, becoming, present, and this the great strength of man: to be always present and to know that he can always be present if he comes to feel that force and to feel himself within it." (*TG* 125.)

Man, then, is himself a perpetual aspiration, transcendence, duration. And although to one living for himself in the horizontal dimension of incomplete being the dead appear to have achieved every possible completion—and thereby cease to long for it—to the poet and mystic the eternal reality is one of which longing and duration are themselves an essential part. The description of the dead young man as a 'single   *192* thirst made single water' is not to be understood, then, as meaning that desire has been converted into satisfaction, but rather that it is now desire *with* satisfaction. Or else—though perhaps this amounts to the same thing—it is a satisfaction which retains the movement of desire, a water whose flow preserves the dynamics of thirst. Here, then, is another aspect of meaning in the paradoxical combination of movement and quietude which the study of the diamond fountain in Chapter II has shown to be so fundamental in all of this poetry. The synthesis of the dynamic and the static represents, in the first instance, a fusion of the temporal and the eternal, but by the same token it symbolizes the fusion of desire with its object, of thirst with water.

We have seen that the "Paraíso" triptych defines eternity as that which continues being what it was, that which is the same, and here, as if to exemplify that definition, the 'different one' is seen in a realm of being in which he is no longer within time, but time is within him, as part of his definitive self, which is now pure reflection or mirage—that is, the pure form and essence of himself. If it is a positive act of 'keeping faith,' the quietude of death is, then, no mere passive inertia, but an intentional projection of a total being from one moment into another. Since the man as an empirical reality possessed such intentionality as an intrinsic component of his essence, the poet perceives intentionality as still intrinsic in that definitive form of being which is the eternal reality of 'having been,' that is, of the in-itself.

The vision which transcends the empirical and phenomenological levels of the poem penetrates, then, to a metaphysical reality which is not subsequent to but contained within real time, and it is for this reason that

that vision is presented parenthetically rather than as the conclusion of the poem. That reality is, then, an eternity immanent within life rather than external to it. The very concept of the eternal within the temporal or of the infinite within the finite is a paradox which by now will seem a familiar one, since we have found it implied in countless images throughout the whole of Jiménez's works. An explicit prose statement of belief in an infinity immanent within life is contained in the *Notes on Poetry and Poetics* written as the poet was entering the seventh decade of his own life:

> I think that this world is our only world, and that in it and with that which is of it, we must accomplish whatever can be accomplished. But why should we not try to make our consciousness contain the infinite universe if it can? The fact that there are poets who have intuitions of infinity is the proof of its existence; and any imagination which is given within man is human. I am sure that in this world in which we live and die there is an immanent transcendency, a moral transcendency, and that the poet is the one who can understand, contain, and express that limitless immanence.[19]

In the most diverse ways, then, Juan Ramón reveals and seeks to satisfy his desire to find a 'sufficient' infinity within the limits of natural existence. Particularly striking is his expression of it in a poem from *Belleza* which sets forth an ideal of life in which the goal is a sufficient qualitative infinity in the dimension of depth—that is, of verticality—intersecting the horizontal dimension of time:

> ¡Grande, tan grande la vida,
> con límites tan sin raya,
> que sea—¡gloria!—mayor
> que la muerte vanidosa!

[19] I translate from a collection of Jiménez's prose writings in the possession of Sr. Don Francisco Hernández-Pinzón Jiménez. It is identified there as being from *Orígenes,* X (1953).

Que la muerte vanidosa
sea sólo el punto negro
—olvido, a veces, no visto—
puesto al fin de su gran luz!
¡Puesto al fin de su gran luz,
punto que no significa;
que no añade más término
a lo que, completo, acaba! (*LP* 1048)

Great, so great be life,
with limits so unbounded,
that it be greater—glory!—than
that vainglorious death!
That vainglorious death
may be only the black point
—forgetting, at times, not seen—
at the end of its great light!
At the end of its great light,
a point which conveys no meaning;
which adds no finality
to that which, complete, is ending!

Life, then, is an autonomous reality, which finds a fulfillment that includes the transcendent and the infinite within natural temporal limits. Death is merely the point that marks the achievement of such fullness, but it has no intrinsic meaning of its own. The concept is essentially that of the Epicureans: Death is nothing to us, for when we are, death is not, and when death is, we are not.

Later in the same book an entirely different interpretation is given to the meaning of death when instead of trying to see it as of null significance for the reality of being which is life, he regards it as a complement to life necessary for the fullness of that being:

Yo no seré yo, muerte,
hasta que tú te unas con mi vida
y me completes así todo;
hasta que mi mitad de luz se cierre

con mi mitad de sombra
—y sea yo equilibrio eterno
en la mente del mundo;
unas veces, mi medio yo, radiante;
otras, mi otro medio yo, en olvido.— (*LP* 1116)

I will not be I, death,
until you unite yourself with my life
and thus make me all complete;
until my half of light is closed
with my half of shadow
—and I am an eternal equilibrium
in the mind of the world;
some times, half of me, in radiance;
other times, my other half, forgotten.

The conceptual means by which he now tries to find death acceptable are so much the extreme opposite of those in the previous poem, that they clearly go even farther than those later formulated into the idea of death as definitive of life. For in this poem he tries to see the fullness of being as achieved not merely through death but actually in and with death, which unites with life to produce that fullness in an 'eternal equilibrium.'

Clearly, though, the consolation is never complete, for the immanent infinity contained in each individual life, though not completely opaque to the poetic vision, does not permit any actual communication with other lives. The loneliness of the 'different one' is still full of poignancy, and his solitude remains hermetic. In another elegiac poem in *La estación total,* he in effect acknowledges that the external intentional projection of the definitive being is still a real loss for the living, for it occurs in a dimension inaccessible to the for-itself. What is more tragic, the eternal light immanent in every consciousness which passes into the in-itself is distinct for each of them, so solitude persists, and there

is a metaphysical depth to what Heidegger would call
the 'unrelatedness'[20] of the dead:

> Perdida en la noche inmensa.
> ¿Quién la encontrará?
> El que muere, cada noche
> más lejos se va.
> Lejos, a la no esperanza.
> Para quien se fué,
> aunque el que se queda implore,
> no vale la fe.
> Y morirnos tras la muerte
> no nos quita cruz,
> que cada muerto camina
> por distinta luz. (*LP* 1209)

> *Lost within the immense night.*
> *By whom will she be found?*
> *Every night, the one who dies*
> *travels farther on.*
> *Farther, in a hopeless realm.*
> *For one who has gone,*
> *though the one who stays beseeches,*
> *faith can not avail.*
> *And our dying after him,*
> *takes no pain away,*
> *for each one who dies must travel*
> *by a distinct light.*

The horizon of time may, then, be accepted as necessary and inevitable in order to give definitive form—
artistic form, one might even say—to life. But there are
still moments when that horizon is regarded chiefly as a
threshold separating light from darkness, and the tragedy of death is not yet overcome.

[20] That is, death itself as the ownmost nonrelational possibility.
(See note 17 above.)

Since the successiveness which Jiménez sees as remaining within being in itself would lead, if its movement were always straight, only to an ever greater isolation of the dead from the living and from each other, it is not surprising that he turned ever more frequently in the later poetry to the concept of circularity as a means by which the desire for eternal successiveness could be harmonized with his wish not to lose what was known and loved in the past. It is, precisely, of a concept rather than of an image or structural principle that we must speak when the circle appears in thematic form as the myth of the eternal return.[1] This theme, which Jiménez once called the myth of poetry itself, makes explicit the desire for temporal infinity which all other manifestations of the circle only implied, and at the same time it offers a means of overcoming that fear of ever-increasing separation expressed in the twelve lines of profound but beautifully ordered emotion in "Perdida en la noche inmensa."

Probably the best expression of the myth is in "Criatura afortunada," one of several poems in *La estación total* in which the coming of spring is celebrated in such terms. The 'fortunate creature' to whom the poem is

[1] Among the papers in the Sala Zenobia y Juan Ramón Jiménez of the Library of the University of Puerto Rico are several notes listing the names of various writers who influenced the poet, particularly in his early years (the title of the note is simply "Fuentes de mi poesía") . Included in one of them is the name of Nietzsche with *mucho* (in parentheses) following it. In all probability Jiménez's acquaintance with the concept of the Eternal Return was a very direct one.

addressed is not specifically named, but the opening verses imply through their own spritely movement as well as in their imagery that the creature is a bird newly returned from its winter refuge:

> Cantando vas, riendo por el agua,
> por el aire silbando vas, riendo,
> en ronda azul y oro, plata y verde. (*LP* 1247)

> *Singing you go, and laughing through the water,*
> *whistling through the air you go, and laughing,*
> *making your rounds, blue and gold, silver and green.*

As the poem progresses, however, the feeling grows that the 'creature' is not merely 'a being' but every being and all of being, and when man contemplates the return and renewal of this creature and all those that accompany it, he is prompted to conceive his own destiny to be that of the eternal return, both by analogy and through the affinity of being with being:

> Nos das la mano, en un momento
> de afinidad posible, de amor súbito,
> de concesión radiante;
> y, a tu contacto cálido,
> en loca vibración de carne y alma,
> nos encendemos de armonía,
> nos olvidamos, nuevos, de lo mismo,
> lucimos, un istante, alegres de oro.
> ¡Parece que también vamos a ser
> perenes como tú,
> que vamos a volar del mar al monte,
> que vamos a saltar del cielo al mar,
> que vamos a volver, volver, volver
> por una eternidad de eternidades!
> ¡Y cantamos, reímos por el aire,
> por el agua reímos y silbamos! (*LP* 1248)

> *You give us your hand, within a moment*
> *of possible affinity, of sudden love,*

200

of radiant concession;
and, at your warm touch,
in wild vibration of our flesh and soul,
we are enkindled with a harmony,
and, being new, forget what is the same,
shining for an instant, gold with joy.
It seems then we shall also be
perennial, like you,
that we shall fly from sea to mountain,
leap from sky to sea,
and shall return, return, return,
through an eternity of eternities!
And we sing, laughing through the air,
through the water we laugh and give our cries!

The final lines of the poem (following those quoted above) recall the opening ones so closely as to suggest a return to the symmetrical structures studied in previous chapters, although here it is so free as to constitute not complete symmetry but simply the coda of a musical rondeau. The similarity is sufficiently marked, however, to constitute a verbal structure expressive itself of the 'return' which is the theme of the conceptual structure.

Even within the mysticism of *Animal de fondo,* there occurs more than once a hint that the God within is to be identified with the child who remains within the heart and mind of the man and that the image of the eternal child-god is ever more vivid in the poet's mind as he approaches the end of his destined existence:

Este encuentro del dios que yo decía,
estaba, como en primavera
primera, de menuda floración,
que en este niñodiós que me esperaba:
el mismo niñodiós que yo fui un día,
que dios fue un día en mi Moguer de España;
mi dios y yo que ya soñábamos con este hoy.

(*LP* 1347)

> *This meeting of the God of which I spoke,*
> *was, as in early spring, of tiny flowering,*
> *within this child-god who was waiting for me:*
> *the same child-god that I was once,*
> *who once was God in my Moguer of Spain;*
> *my God and I who then were dreaming of this day.*[2]

Juan Ramón had once said in an aphorism that the best symbol of eternity is the "present" for a child, and perhaps it is the quality of eternity in every moment of the life of a child which makes him seem divine.[3] It is clear, in any case, that in the vision of the child-god is implied a cyclic concept of life, for although that vision is intrinsically retrospective, everything in the poem implies that the achievement of it has been the goal of the poet's entire life, that the years of childhood in Moguer are now becoming a *temps retrouvé,* and that death will mark the completion of a circle whose end touches its beginning.

In one of the posthumously published poems in the edition of Sánchez-Barbudo, there is expressed even more explicitly the idea of a return to the beginning, a beginning which is also the end:

> Como en el infinito, Dios,
> Vuelvo a tu orijen (tu orijen que es mi fin)
> y quizá a tu fin, sin nada de ese enmedio
> que las jentes te han puesto encima
> de tu sola, tu limpia luz. (*DDD* 220)

> *As in infinity, God,*
> *I return to your beginning (your beginning which is*
> *my end)*

---

[2] The fourth line of the original poem begins with a "que" which I have not attempted to include in the translation. (In his edition of *Dios deseado y deseante* (p. 139), Sánchez-Barbudo suggests that its presence may be an error.)

[3] *La colina de los chopos,* p. 116.

and perhaps to your end, with nothing of that in-
    between
which men have laid upon
your single, limpid light.

More explicit, too, is the idea expressed later in the
same poem that the return to the child-god is a preparation for death—one might almost say preparation for a
good death:

> Una blanca hoja,
> reflejo de una mente en blanco,
> eres tú para mí, y en ella tú palpitas
> con color de mi tiempo, desde aquel niñodiós
> que en mi Moguer de España fui yo un día,
> hasta este niñodiós que quiero otra vez ser
> para morir, el nuevo siempre;
> el que el niño comprende como niño,
> sin interés ninguno,
> como en el infinito, Dios nuestro infinito
>
> (*DDD* 221)

> *A white page,*
> *reflection of a limpid mind,*
> *are you for me, in which you palpitate*
> *with all the color of my time, from that child-god*
> *who once in my Moguer of Spain was I,*
> *to this child-god I wish again to be*
> *that I may die, forever new;*
> *one the child understands as child,*
> *disinterested,*
> *as in infinity, God, our infinity.*

The desire is similar, certainly, to one frequently
expressed by Unamuno, as for example in the poem
Teresa:

> Tú, Señor, que a Dios hiciste niño,
> hazme niño al morirme.

Thou, Lord, who of God didst make a child,
make me a child upon my death.

There can be no doubt that Jiménez was well aware of many such utterances in Unamuno, but in a desire so profoundly felt it is pointless even to speak of 'influences.' In any case the poet from Moguer differs from Unamuno in his explicit incorporation of the desire into the concept of the Eternal Return, for it is typical of both of them that whereas Unamuno's horror of death prompted him to express such desires at the same time that his reason rejected all intellectual grounds for believing in the possibility of their fulfillment, Jiménez expressed them in the context of an intellectual construct which is convincing because it justifies itself aesthetically.[4]

Such a construct is not, then, the result of any rational process but is prompted by Jiménez's conception

[4] See the discussion of the meanings of childhood for Unamuno in Carlos Blanco Aguinaga, *El Unamuno contemplativo* (México, 1959), pp. 97–111, to which I am also indebted for the example. Apropos of what we have said above in comparing and contrasting Jiménez and Unamuno, it is well to mention also the very acute observations of José Olivio Jiménez in a recent book on poetry and time. Of Unamuno and Machado he says that they also "se rebelaban, cada uno a su manera, ante la inexorabilidad del tiempo; pero al hacerlo estaban continuamente invocándolo, dejándose atravesar directamente por esa misma inquietud, nombrándolo, y de forma muy concreta." But Jiménez, in contrast, "aunque nunca dejará de expresar su asombro dolorido ante la nada que circunda a la existencia, trató siempre, en lo posible, de salvar los escollos de la contingencia directa, es decir, de lo que a él le pareciera burdamente accidental. Y en aras de esa esencialidad total que se había impuesto, intentó y logró en elevadísimos momentos extraer la pura y desnuda verdad que las cosas le ocultaban como un reto." José Olivio Jiménez, *Cinco poetas del tiempo* (Madrid, 1964), p. 20. I would only add that—as I hope to show at the end of this chapter—the 'pure and naked truth' of things proves for Juan Ramón to be also intrinsically temporal and dynamic.

of the nature of poetry itself. In previous chapters we have seen how the circle and the circularity implied in symmetrical structures are symbols of the poet's search for the ideal beauty central to all things, of the attitude of lyric reflection, and of the *éstasis dinámico* which is the very substance of poetry. It is for this reason, chiefly, that the concept of cyclic time, the myth of the Eternal Return, is regarded as intrinsic in all poetry. For this reason, too, he often regards his poetic work as a center about which the circle of his life is organized and from which it may, in a sense, be said to emanate. Such, for example, is the meaning for him of the brief poem by Goethe, the first lines of which appear at the beginning of each of his books from *Poesía* (1923) to *La estación total* (1946):

> Wie das Gestirn,
> Ohne Hast,
> Aber ohne Rast,
> Drehe sich jeder
> Um die eigne Last.
>
> *Like the stars,*
> *without haste,*
> *but without rest,*
> *each man must circle*
> *round his own task.*

In other moments, poetry is not the center but rather the body moving in orbit, either around the poet's consciousness,[5] or simply as part of the movement of the

[5] An example of this is in a draft of manuscript of the prologue to the anthology, *Canción* (which was actually published in 1936 with no prologue whatsoever). It begins: "Considero actualmente mi obra poética como un cuerpo desprendido de mí mismo, que jira por su órbita fatal (con el agobio del coro de sus satélites salidos de ella) alrededor de mí." The manuscript is among the papers con-

whole of reality through time and space. The latter view is clearly expressed in Juan Ramón's answer to a question from the literary review *Caracola,* which asked whether poetry has an orbit independent from the rest of human culture. To this he replied:

Everything, world and man, revolves in a single orbit, and there is no more than one orbit for all things and all men, the orbit of time in space. And the orbit of poetry is that of life itself, man and world. To revolve in the orbit is to make poetry, because it is to undergo metamorphosis, in infinite successiveness. If an authentic poet lived forever, his poetry would be always the same and always different, in every age, and that is what poetry is in every age, for a poet ought to signify all of the past and all of the future.[6]

It is significant that where the questioner had used the word 'orbit' in a basically conventional sense, the metaphor having been weakened to meaning little more than 'place,' the poet's answer seizes upon the literal meaning of the word, restores the idiom to the condition of a poetic metaphor, and presents it as an objective fact of cosmic reality.

These three ways of conceiving the relation between poetry and life—the life of the poet and the life of all of humanity—are clearly distinct from each other, but since they are all based upon the same fundamental image of the circle, it is natural to think of them as simultaneously present in each appearance of the image. As we have seen in more than one instance previously, it is part of the intrinsic paradox of the

---

tained in the Library of the University of Puerto Rico. The ill-humored reference to those he regarded as ungrateful imitators is probably the reason he discarded this beginning in a better moment, and apparently never returned to the project.

[6] Published first in *Caracola* in April, 1954. (I quote the passage as reprinted in *La corriente infinita,* p. 221.)

circle that the circumference and center are each contained in the other, and therefore as symbols their
meanings, too, are readily exchanged. In some sense, in
fact, the third appearance of the image is a synthesis of
the meanings of the previous two.

If it is within and through poetry that the reality of
life is given coherence in the image of circle and center,
poetry is also the means by which Jiménez achieves and
possesses a vision of the ultimate beauty to which in
Animal de fondo he gives the name God. As he writes in
the notes to that book, "Today I think that I have not
labored in vain in God, that I have labored in God to
the extent that I have labored in poetry." (*LP* 1344)
Once the vision is achieved, however, it is autonomous,
and the relation of its object to the poet's subjective
consciousness is distinct from that of the relation between poetry and life, although embodied in the same
structural concept of circle and center:

> Cuando sales en sol, dios conseguido,
> no estás en el nacerte sólo;
> estás en el ponerte,
> en mi norte, en mi sur;
> estás, con los matices de una cara grana,
> interior y completa,
> que mira para dentro,
> en la totalidad del tiempo y el espacio.
>   Y yo estoy dentro de ella,
> dentro de tu conciencia jeneral estoy
> y soy tu secreto, tu diamante,
> tu tesoro mayor, tu ente entrañable. (*LP* 1354)

> *When you come with the sun, oh God achieved,*
> *you are not only in your place of rising;*
> *you are in your setting,*
> *in my north, in my south;*
> *you are, with the nuances of a scarlet face,*
> *which is internal and complete,*

207

> *which looks within,*
> *in the totality of time and space.*
> *And I am in that totality,*
> *within your general consciousness am I,*
> *I am your secret and your diamond,*
> *your chief treasure, and inmost being.*

In this poem the circle of the God achieved is very evidently one of simultaneity, with divinity present in every point of the compass surrounding the subjective consciousness. But just as the triptych in *La estación total* had presented a view of eternity as successiveness—as well, that is, as constituting a timeless simultaneous present—so there occurs in *Animal de fondo* a concept of God Himself as successiveness. The prose poem which concludes the portion of that series published before Jiménez's death expresses it clearly:

> Tú eres el sucesivo, lo sucesivo eres; lo que siempre vendrá, el que siempre vendrá; que eres el ansia abstracta, la que nunca se fina, porque el recuerdo tuyo es vida tanto como tú. (*LP* 1356)

> *You are the successive one; you are what is successive; that which will always come; the one who will always come; for you are the abstract longing; one which is never ended, for your memory is life as much as you.*

So fundamental is the kinetic quality in the poet's sense of what the world is (one must speak here of intuitive sense rather than of rational understanding) that it is projected by his poetic imagination beyond the limits of the known world into the realm of the eternal and the divine. In the rarified atmosphere of *Animal de fondo*, from which virtually all familiar images have been cast out, the sense of *sucesión*, of time itself, is the one phenomenon common to all human experience which most immediately and insistently reveals itself as persisting within Juan Ramón's metaphysical universe. It must be remembered, therefore, that even the concept of simultaneity and the symbolization of it in the circle actually represents the sum of all moments of successiveness, whose number is infinite.

If, then, we look back upon the individual images and total 'compositions of place' in the early poetry, it will be realized all the more clearly that the static vision so frequent there (and of which much has had to be said in every portion of this study), far from expressing an absolute timelessness, was itself a means by which Jiménez came to express the dynamism of internal time-consciousness.[7] In a static image like that of the diamond fountain, the suppression of nearly all visible movement could, indeed, abolish the empirical time which is the number of motion, but it thereby succeeded, as nothing else could, in rendering perceptible the flow of pure internal time, pure human time.

The static image was doubtless the principal means by which Jiménez sought to capture the timeless essences of the objects of experience, but its usual effect was only to heighten the sense of temporality in his poetry. It must, then, be concluded from our study that within and behind the "statisches Weltgefühl" which Emmy Neddermann so admirably documented there is

---

[7] The static vision constitutes, then, the unity of a stream of lived experience, a unity within the temporal flux of which it may be said, with Husserl, that it "is originally constituted through the fact of the flux itself; that is, its true essence is not only to be, in general, but to be a unity of lived experience and to be given in internal consciousness." I quote Edmund Husserl, *The Phenomenology of Internal Time-Consciousness*, trans. James S. Churchill (Bloomington, Ind.; 1964), p. 157.

a sense of the world which is profoundly and completely temporal.

It must, in fact, be granted that this all-pervasive temporality is the chief source of Jiménez's difficulty in attaining to the essential reality of objects, and this, in turn, is the principal limitation in the scope of his poetic vision. The criticisms of his poetry made in recent years by the late Luis Cernuda are so filled with personal rancor as to be always suspect, but there is certainly some truth to his charge that Jiménez's impressionism is the result of a lack of curiosity concerning the inner reality of the objects of sense experience.[8] What is true in the charge is simply the objective fact that Jiménez's poetry does not, actually, often capture that reality, which simply means that it is profoundly intimate, personal, subjective—in a word, lyrical. Rather than due to a lack of curiosity, however, it must be recognized as a difficulty resulting from the corrosive effects of his sense of time. His concentration upon the sense impression of a given moment is in reality the effect of his skepticism and even despair concerning the very possibility of discovering in retrospect and preserving in memory the inner reality of an entity which had charmed him in a 'present' that has now become past. As one of the *Sonetos espirituales* expressed it:

> ¿Cómo era, Dios mío, cómo era?
> —¡Oh, corazón falaz, mente indecisa!—
> ¿Era como el pasaje de la brisa?
> ¿Como la huida de la primavera? . . .
>   Todo tu cambiar trocóse en nada

---

[8] Cernuda, *Estudios,* p. 123. (See also chap. IV, note 20, of this work.

—¡memoria, ciega abeja de amargura!—
¡No sé cómo eras, yo que sé que fuiste! (*LP* 26)

> *What was it like, oh God, what was it like?*
> *Oh, deceitful heart, mind in confusion!*
> *Was it like the passing of a breeze?*
> *Or like the flight of spring? . . .*
> *All of this changing turned to nothingness*
> *—oh, memory, blind bee of bitterness!—*
> *I do not know what you were like, but only that you*
> *were!*

Such anxiety could never have been the result of
indifference to the inner reality of a phenomenon. It is
due, rather, precisely to the intensity of Jiménez's desire
to seize that inner reality, the essence of the object of
experience (expressed in the question by using a form
of the verb *ser,* which refers to the substantial being of
things) seen as drifting off into the past with the inexorable flow of time. If it be argued that his concern here
is not with the object itself but only with his experience
of it, we must still insist that it is his sense of time and a
Heraclitean pessimism derived from it which makes
him feel that the object *now* is simply not the same as
the object *then.*

One cannot, in any case, doubt the earnestness of
Juan Ramón's desire to contemplate things in themselves or deny that he ever attained to such a vision of
them. The most notable expression of that desire is in a
well known poem from *Eternidades* which actually
might serve as a basic *ars poetica* for a poetry of "things
as they are" like that which has gained prominence in
Spain since the end of the Civil War:

> ¡Intelijencia, dame
> el nombre esacto de las cosas!
> Que mi palabra sea

la cosa misma,
creada por mi alma nuevamente.
Que por mí vayan todos
los que no las conocen, a las cosas;
que por mí vayan todos
los que ya las olvidan, a las cosas;
que por mí vayan todos
los mismos que las aman, a las cosas. . . (*LP* 553)

Intellect, give me
the precise name of things!
*   May my word be*
the thing itself,
newly created by my soul.
By me, may all
who do not know them come to things;
By me, may all who already forget them come to things;
By me, may all
Those who love them come to things.

It can scarcely be denied that the attitude in these lines is fundamentally an objective one, and if a note of subjective impressionism seems to persist in the reference to the 'thing' as created by the poet's soul, this can probably be understood as meaning simply that word and object are so closely identified that the newly created poetic word endues the object itself with the newness of recent creation. But however important poetry may be in naming—that is, in defining and identifying—things, it is the things themselves which are here regarded as the ultimate objects of cognition and of love. This is, then, a poetic ideal sincerely felt and admirably expressed, but it must be granted that it did not, in fact, become the basis for a poetry of the object in Jiménez's work itself. His constant preoccupation with time made it inevitable that his principal esthetic ideal should be that of *éstasis dinámico.*

But this does not mean that the former ideal never found any expression whatever in Jiménez's works. There is, for example, a very striking poem, written, presumably, in the spring of 1945 (just before the period of *Animal de fondo*), in which the poet's sense of the autonomous reality of the objects of nature is very movingly expressed:

> El sauce y el almendro
> que vimos esta tarde en Kenwood,
> allí estarán pasando su belleza
> esta noche de primavera viva,
> sin verse el uno al otro,
> sin ellos mismos verse,
> sin saber estos nombres que les damos,
> sin ser vistos de nadie,
> sin pájaro en su sitio;
> el sauce casi verde, el casi blanco almendro
> (verdoso, sonrosado)
> entre la lenta bruma del bosque de colinas,
> troncos, troncos y troncos negros,
> hacia el poniente grana y amarillo.
>   Cada segundo
> de aquel preciso ser y estar en flor y en hoja,
> copiados por el lento riachuelillo
> como el poniente grana y amarillo,
> será una gracia nueva
> de línea y de color,
> de olor y toque,
> de sabor y de oído,
> en esta vaga luna que al sol ha sucedido. . .

> *The willow and the almond tree*
> *which we saw this afternoon in Kenwood,*
> *will still be there, passing their time of beauty,*
> *within this night of living spring,*
> *not seeing one another,*
> *without seeing themselves,*
> *without knowing these names we give to them,* 213

and being seen by no one,
with no bird in its place;
the willow almost green, the almond almost white
(but with a hint of green and pink),
amid the slow mist of wooded hills,
innumerable black trunks of other trees,
against the sunset of scarlet and gold.
  Each second of
that precise truth and fact of being in flower and leaf,
copied by the slowly moving brook,
as is the sunset of scarlet and gold,
will be a new grace
of line and color,
of odor and touch,
of taste and sound,
within this vague moonlight which has followed the
  sun. . .

The objective view of the substantial being and the factual existence of the two trees (a distinction expressed in Spanish through the substantival use of the verbs *ser* and *estar,* and rendered in the translation by 'the truth and fact of being') is completely independent, then, of the names given to them and of all the words used to describe them, and in his recognition of that independence, the poet achieves an intuition into what is at once the most immediate and the most profound truth concerning these and all objects: that they are *there.* Nothing, then, could be farther than this poem from the solipsistic subjectivism of which Cernuda accuses Jiménez.

This is all the more notable because in so many ways the poem seems absolutely typical of Jiménez's impressionism. The scarlet and gold of the sunset and the delicate tones of green, white and pink bring to mind the painterly impressionism of Renoir and Manet, and harken back to the colorism of the first poetic period, *214* the 'almost' used to describe the colors of the trees being virtually the key to the aesthetics of that period. Certainly much emphasis is also given to the impression which those objects made upon the senses—and to that which they *would* make if there were anyone to watch them by moonlight—but the chief concern of the poem is with the fact of their autonomous being and existence as objects, regardless of the presence of any subjective consciousness by which they are perceived. It is almost as though he were perceiving this truth for the first time at the age of sixty-three, for there is a quality of child-like wonder in his expression of this simple but profoundly significant fact. In creating this quality he is, of course, performing a primary function of both the poet and the philosopher: to make the familiar seem strange and the strange familiar.

An immediate corollary of the intuition into the autonomous reality of objects is the realization that as pure objects they have no consciousness of each other or of themselves, and therefore they are of being in-itself. Yet they also are a fact of being in a particular time and place, and possess a fluid successiveness of which the poet is acutely aware: they are 'passing their time of beauty' second by second. But despite their limited temporal existence, there is nothing of the consciously projected or self-transcending being for-itself in them; their absolute objectivity is possible only because of their absolute lack of consciousness. In the last lines of the poem, their state of being is compared and contrasted with that of the poet himself, thereby making strikingly clear the polar contrast between subject and object. This occurs within the context of a familiar pattern of repetition reminiscent of, but never actually imitating, the symmetry of earlier poems:

Cada segundo suyo,
cada segundo mío,
perdiendo su belleza,
pasando mi sentido,
el sauce y el almendro
que vimos esta tarde en Kenwood,
sin pájaro en su sitio;
troncos y troncos negros
contra el poniente grana y amarillo. *(LP* 928)

Each second of their time,
each second of mine,
they, losing their beauty,
I, spending conscious sense,
the willow and the almond tree
which we saw this afternoon in Kenwood,
with no bird in its place;
so many black trunks of other trees
against the sunset of scarlet and gold.

This degree of subjectivity is not a return to solipsism but is essential to the establishment of the polarity, for the awareness of self as self is inseparable from the awareness of object as object, and solipsism is precisely the state in which the two are no longer distinct. Ultimately, in fact, it may be seen that the definition of this polarity constitutes the principal achievement of the poem, for through it the cognitive experience of objects seen during a stroll through the Maryland countryside is not swept away in the subsequent passing of time. Having recognized their autonomous reality, he no longer needs to ask anxiously what they were like, as he did in the sonnet quoted earlier. A single moment's recognition of their existence as objects also revealed the truth of their being as objects, and this truth is their essence, which is eternal.[9]

[9] In his commentary on the "ser y estar en flor y hoja," Don Basilio de Pablos recalls the traditional philosophical distinction between the two basic types of movement: "Pero hay dos clases

When Jiménez does not achieve such a sense of the object—and it must be admitted that the achievement of it is relatively rare in his poetry—there is, certainly, a limitation in the breadth of his poetic world and in the scope of human experiences which it expresses, and the result is a poetry which is musical rather than imagistic, concerned with time rather than with history, and onto-logical rather than existential. But it would be difficult to deny the priority in poetry and in human thought of the first member of each of these dualities, and it may, perhaps, be said that the most fundamental way in which Jiménez's work was a *poesía pura* is that it is basic poetry, a 'first poetry' whose themes are the prob-lems of the 'first philosophy.' Certainly this results at times in a high degree of abstraction, but this is not at all the same as dehumanization. In the statement quoted in Chapter V concerning his belief in an immanent infinity, he had said that "any imagination given within man is human." And to this it might be added that his temporal anxiety and longing to attain to essences are thoroughly human emotions and therefore alien to no man.

It is clear that Jiménez's lifelong search for an ideal beauty, which in *Animal de fondo* achieves its goal and

---

de movimiento: el espacial, exterior, y el metafísico o inmanente. El movimiento espacial es el menos profundo. En un plano más íntimo están los cambios formales: cualitativo-cuantitativos. Y en el plano más hondo el movimiento esencial." He rightly sees this 'essential movement' as the kind present in the intuition and po-etic imagery of Jiménez, and it is this which gives the internal dynamism to his static vision. Concerning the point of view in the poem here discussed, cf. the one in *TA* 927–28 and the commentary on it by Howard T. Young in *The Victorious Expression*, pp. 122–23. For the concepts of 'truth of being' and 'fact of being' see the article on *Esencia* in José Ferrater Mora, *Diccionario de filo-sofía* (Buenos Aires, 1958).

to which, once achieved, he gives the name of God, is also, at the most fundamental level, a search for essence, for the inner reality of things which, precisely because it is reality, is eternal. The reference here to 'things' means, of course, all things, and to that total essence can be given also the name of Being.

The equivalence of the two goals is made clear in a retrospective poem in which Juan Ramón compares his state following the mystic experience on his sea voyage with that of the self of former years. He realizes that nothing has changed except his own understanding of the true relation between God and the self:

> Entre aquellos jeranios, bajo aquel limón,
> junto a aquel pozo, con aquella niña,
> tu luz estaba allí, dios deseante;
> tú estabas a mi lado,
> dios deseado,
> pero no habías entrado todavía en mí.
> (*LP* 1331, *Animal de fondo*)

> *Among those geraniums, under that lemon tree,*
> *beside that well, with that girl-child,*
> *your light was there, desiring God;*
> *and you were at my side,*
> *Oh God desired,*
> *but had not entered yet in me.*

Then follows an explicit reference to a poem from *Piedra y cielo* which was quoted in the previous chapter as one of the most memorable expressions of Jiménez's constant pursuit of beauty and of his inability ever to possess it fully. It is the poem in which beauty is a "butterfly of light," which always escapes, leaving the poet only with the "form of its flight":

> El sol, el azul, el oro eran,
> como la luna y las estrellas,
> tu chispear y tu coloración completa,

pero yo no podía cojerte con tu esencia,
la esencia se me iba
(como la mariposa de la forma)
porque la forma estaba en mí
y al correr tras lo otro la dejaba;
tanto, tan fiel que la llevaba,
que no me parecía lo que era. (*LP* 1332)

The sun, the blue, the gold all were,
as were the moon and stars,
your scintillation and color complete,
but I could not seize you with your essence,
the essence fled from me
(as did the butterfly of the form)
because the form was in me,
and running after other things I left it behind;
so much, so faithfully I bore it,
that it did not seem to me what it was.

In contrast to that former state, he is now able to declare his complete possession of that essence, which he has gained by means of a revelation which is as mysterious as it is unexpected:

Y hoy, así, sin yo saber por qué,
la tengo entera, entera.
No sé qué día fué ni con qué luz
vino a un jardín, tal vez, casa mar, monte,
y vi que era mi nombre sin mi nombre,
sin mi sombra, mi nombre,
el nombre que yo tuve antes de ser
oculto en este ser que me cansaba,
porque no era este ser que hoy he fijado
(que pude no fijar)
para todo el futuro iluminado
iluminante,
dios deseado y deseante. (*LP* 1332)

And now, just so, without my knowing why,
I have it complete, complete.
I do not know what day it was nor with what light
it came into a garden, perhaps, house, sea, mountain,
and I saw it was my name without my name,

> *without my shadow, my name,*
> *one I had before I was*
> *hidden in this being I was weary of,*
> *because it was not this being which I now have secured*
> *(but might never have secured)*
> *for all the future, illuminated*
> *and illuminating,*
> *God, desired and desiring.*

Although it was said in the first part of the poem that until the moment of revelation God had not yet entered the poet's consciousness, it becomes clear in the central section that the 'form' within is the same as the essence which he had been seeking, but the anxious search for it in things external to and beyond his own mind only carried him farther from it. The final apprehension of that essence was effected by a simple act of cognition— which appears to the seeker much like a special revelation—of the truth that the essence he had sought was within him all the while. The discovery of the Divine or Absolute Essence thus coincides with the discovery of his own essence, and he thereby realizes that in searching for one he was at the same time seeking the other.

In acknowledging the identity of the two essences, he approaches that form of mysticism which has found its fullest expression in the *Upanishads*, where that identity is proclaimed in the formula, *Tat tvam asi*, 'That art thou.'[10] It is a formula which expresses the concept of

[10] As, for example, in Hume's translation of the *Thirteen Principal Upanishads*, p. 249: "That which is the finest essence—this whole world has that as its soul. That is Reality. That is Atman (Soul). That art thou, Svetaketu." In Jiménez another example of a similar concept can be found in the last lines of his prologue to the *Diario*, where he speaks of his soul as "tied to the center of the one by an elastic thread of grace; poor soul of great wealth, which going toward what was its own, thought it was going to some other thing . . ." (*LP* 204).

identity between the human and the divine, the subjective and the transcendent, and between the self and
Self—which is the form of identity most specifically
referred to in the formula and in Hindu philosophy's
concept of Divine Essence as *Atman,* the Self. Yet
despite the strong probability of a direct influence from
Eastern thought in Jiménez's spiritual attitudes, they
can perhaps be more clearly understood in terms of
recent Western philosophy's ontological analyses than
of oriental mysticism, not simply because the former
provides a reductionist explanation for the latter, but
because Jiménez was always so rationalistic and secular
in his thinking as to remain basically within the Western tradition. It is not surprising, then, if we see in his
vision of a longed-for identity of self with Self an
intuition similar to that of the ontological analyses of
consciousness in Hegel and Sartre,[11] for there is no
European poet in whose work the immediate structure
of consciousness as an anguished awareness of separation
of the self from its own being, of failing to be what it is
is more clearly evident; and in Jiménez's poetic version
of the *Tat tvam asi* is immediately implied the goal of
every conscious subject: to coincide with its own being.
For despite the distance separating it from that being,
the latter is completely its own, and when we write here
of an ideal identity of self with Self it must be understood that the honorific capital refers not to a being
actually distinct from the 'self,' but only to the self seen
as a goal which for consciousness is forever transcendent

---

[11] Sartre's analyses have already been mentioned in the previous
chapter, but since we speak here of a certain Western 'tradition,'
it is well to refer also to the analysis presented in the first two parts
of Hegel's *Phenomenology of Mind,* which influenced Sartre so
profoundly.

—that is, just beyond reach—and therefore ever desired, loved, and revered.

In order to understand that 'truth of being' which is the *esencia* spoken of in the central section of the poem, one must recognize the 'butterfly of the form' as an allusion to the famous poem from *Piedra y cielo* (quoted in Chapter IV), in which beauty is a 'butterfly of light' that always eludes the poet's grasp, leaving him only with the 'form of its flight.' The evocation of this last concept makes it evident that here, too, the word 'form' and the 'essence' with which it is equated must be understood as meaning the 'form of flight.' At the end, therefore, of Jiménez's lifelong search for the inner reality of things, of himself, and of God, he perceives it, not as inert substance or as purely static being, but as dynamic form, a structure of movement.

Before the period of *Animal de fondo,* the very word 'essence' was a relatively rare one in Jiménez's poetry, being used most frequently to mean simply 'fragrance' in a flower and only secondarily referring to the whole quality of being of the flower itself. In the last book, however, the term is very clearly established as one of several equivalent names for the *dios deseado y deseante:*

> Cada mañana veo la ciudad
> donde te hallé del todo, dios, esencia,
> conciencia, tú, hermosura llena. (*LP* 1349)
>
> *Each morning I see the city*
> *where I found you completely, God—essence,*
> *consciousness, you, and complete beauty.*

In another poem the temporal dynamism which is the essence of God—and of man—is endued with the quietude of eternity by the poet's sense of the simultaneous presence of all objects of experience and of time as the sum total of all its successive moments:

> En estas perspectivas ciudadales
> que la vida suceden, como prismas,
> con su sangre de tiempo en el cojido espacio,
> tú, conciencia de dios, eres presente fijo,
> esencia tesorera de dios mío,
> con todas las edades
> de colores, de músicas, de voces,
> en país de países. (*LP* 1333)

> *In perspectives like these, as though of cities*
> *that give a prism-like successiveness to life*
> *with its temporal blood in captured space,*
> *you, consciousness of God, are a fixed present,*
> *treasuring essence of my God,*
> *with all ages*
> *of colors, music, voices,*
> *in a realm of realms.*

It is not difficult, in this abstract image of the spectrum seen in a 'city-like' perspective, to recognize the continuing presence of the sunset scene, of inexhaustible fascination for the impressionist poet. But the ordering of every nuance of the sunset's colors into the prismatic gamut is essential for the creation from such a scene of a symbol of temporal successiveness, a creation effected with the image—poignant, but conceptually bold—of the "sangre de tiempo en el cojido espacio." The representation of successiveness by means of this symbol confers an immediate simultaneity upon each point in the series, and the space which is 'captured' in the single glance of a beholder's eye represents by analogy the whole of a temporal series likewise 'captured' in a single comtemplative moment. The 'treasuring essence' which is the 'consciousness of God' (a phrase understood here as a subjective rather than objective genitive, although the ambiguity is doubtless deliberate) accumulates and preserves within itself the content of each moment of that series in the vision of an eternal and simultaneous present which orthodox theology regards as a prime attribute of God and to which the mystic and every true believer aspire. In poetry, that vision is achieved through the spatialization of time, which in these verses is so complete as to create a realm in which are found simultaneously every age of past and future history and every sight and sound—all sense experiences—which they have contained. Such a realm is necessarily eternal—*is* eternity itself, and therefore it is a 'realm of realms,' a spatial symbol of the *saecula saeculorum*.

The temporal successiveness thus seen is, despite the simultaneity and the cumulative faculty of the vision, correlative to the successiveness which is in consciousness itself, whether human or divine. This is the concept set forth at the beginning of the second stanza, which in its first line refers again to the "perspectivas ciudadales":

> Y en ellas, simultánea
> creencia de fijados paraísos de fondo,
> te sucedes también, conciencia y dios
> intercalado de verdores nuevos,
> de niñas de color solar,
> de cobre retenido en adiós largo,
> que componen tu sólita estación total,
> tu intemporalidad tan realizada en mí. (*LP* 1333)

> *And in them, simultaneous*
> *belief in fixed paradises of depth,*
> *you succeed yourself also, consciousness and God,*
> *interpolated with new greens,*

224

with children of the color of the sun,
with copper retained in a long farewell,
which compose your constant total season,
your timelessness so realized in me.

If the attribution of successiveness to the divine consciousness is much less 'orthodox' than was concept of simultaneity in the divine vision, it can be immediately added that the simultaneity of summation is found as much in that subjective successiveness which is consciousness as it was in the successiveness of the object.[12] So close, indeed, is the parallel, that, as we have seen elsewhere in *Animal de fondo,* the distinction between subject and object is virtually lost, and the divine consciousness is described as 'interpolated' successively with the new greens of returning springs, colors of children in the summer sun, and copper hues of autumn leaves and sunsets, all of which would presumably have been thought to be attributes of the natural world which is the object of consciousness, rather than of the Mind which is its subject. The implication of this virtual identification of the two poles of consciousness is that divinity is immanent in the world itself, a subjectivity constituted by its objects. Therefore the successiveness of objective consciousness of time, and the summation of the temporal series is constitutive of a 'constant total

[12] Although it is natural to compare Jiménez's spiritual ideas to those of orthodox religion, I naturally do not mean to suggest that orthodoxy was at all his concern. A very useful summary and study of Jiménez's religious thought is presented in the thesis of Carlos del Saz-Orozco SJ, *Desarrollo del concepto de Dios en el pensamiento de Juan Ramón Jiménez* (Madrid, 1966), in which it is asserted that Jiménez's God "no es el Dios cristiano; sino una divinidad en conciencia universal, para quien el poeta crea en su interior un mundo interno de belleza externa, centrado en un nombre: Dios 'El nombre conseguido de los nombres' (p. 214)."

season,' a timelessness realized in a consciousness which is total, and in which the poet shares.

It is, however, the final poem in the *Libros de poesía* which most explicitly proclaims dynamic temporality to be the essence of divinity and reaffirms the *panta rhei* as the ultimate truth in a world composed of pure color, light, and rhythmic successiveness. As in all the poems of *Animal de fondo,* the second person singular refers to the *dios deseado y deseante.* The first part of the prose poem was quoted earlier in this chapter, and the work ends on a note of almost pure temporality:

> Sí; en masa de verdad reveladora, de sucesión perpetua pasas, en masa de color, de luz, de ritmo; en densidad de amor estás pasando, estás viniendo, estás presente siempre; pasando estás en mí; eres lo ilimitado de mi órbita.
>
> Y me detengo en mi alijeración, porque en el horizonte del espacio eterno estás cayendo siempre hasta mi imán. Tu sucesión no es fuga de lo mío, es venida impetuosa de lo tuyo, del todo que eres tú, eterno vividor del todo; caminante y camino a fuerza de pasado, a fuerza de presente, a fuerza de futuro.
>
> (*LP* 1356)

> *Yes; in a body of revealing truth, of perpetual successiveness you pass, in body of color, light, and rhythm; in density and love you pass, you come, you are ever present; and are passing within me; you are what is limitless in my orbit.*
>
> *And I stop in my acceleration, because in the horizon of eternal space you are always falling to my magnet. Your own successiveness is no flight from what is mine, it is impetuous coming from what is yours, from the all which is you, eternal force of life in all; wayfarer and way by force of past, by force of present, and by force of future.*

The God within is no mere static 'presence' but a constant coming from the infinitely distant horizon to

226

the center of the poet's consciousness, and this infinite coming is what gives an immanent infinity to the orbit—the circle—of his own life. Ultimately, however, the dynamism or 'acceleration' of that circle is superseded by the impetuous successiveness of the eternal force of life, the *vividor* which not only lives within all things but far and beyond them as well. So thoroughly is subjective consciousness absorbed into this vision of metaphysical dynamism that it now feels no anguish for the eventual loss of its own finite existence, or even any awareness that its actual absorption into the infinite implies such a loss. Only in the over-whelming dynamic presence of divine totality can Jiménez find satisfaction for what he once called his "total anhelo," 'total longing,' which here is clearly seen to be for the whole of time. For the God desired and desiring is both wayfarer —the power which moves through time and space— and way—the abiding form of movement which unites past, present, and future into a single eternal reality.

In these lines, which conclude the volume of *Libros de poesía,* we discover that the conscious awareness of this reality is identical with the consciousness of God, who in the form of wayfarer and way is the supreme manifestation of the synthesis of time and the timeless, of *éstasis dinámico,* which is the central theme of our study. The name of God is given to that ultimate reality because the poet regards it, with love, as a Thou, which in its ontological structure so fully includes (at the same time that it transcends) the structure of conciousness, that it is itself conscious—itself an I as well as a Thou. And that structure, which is an eternal becoming, an eternal but never definitive realization of being by consciousness, is the essence for which Jiménez had always sought:

227

Tú, esencia, eres conciencia; mi conciencia
y la de otros, la de todos,
con forma suma de conciencia;
que la esencia es lo sumo,
es la forma suprema conseguible,
y tu esencia está en mí, como mi forma. (*LP* 1290)

You, essence, are consciousness, my consciousness
and that of others, that of everyone,
with supreme form of consciousness;
for essence is what is supreme,
the highest form achievable,
and your essence is within me, as my form.

The peril of absolute subjectivity, by which Jiménez the contemplative poet and mystic had so often been beset, is at length overcome through the universalizing and sharing of consciousness, so that his metaphysics becomes, rather, an absolute humanism—absolute and essential, for consciousness is the essence of what is human. The God of Juan Ramón is, then, the absolute and universal form of the ontological structure of man himself and of that to which he aspires, a synthesis of existence and essence, being which is at once in and for itself.

Logically, perhaps, such syntheses are either impossible or possible only if the term is taken in the etymological sense of a 'simultaneous positing,' as we have seen in all of Jiménez's paradoxes. In Sartre, for example, we find an absolute insistence upon the impossibility of synthesis as fusion between the in-itself and the for-itself, but in many ways his analysis of the ontological aspiration of human consciousness describes perfectly what Jiménez's vision seeks to achieve:

This perpetually absent being which haunts the for-itself is itself fixed in the in-itself. It is the impossible synthesis of the for-itself and the in-itself; it would be its own foundation not as nothingness but as being and would preserve within it the necessary translucency of consciousness along with the coincidence with itself of being in-itself. It would preserve in it that turning back upon the self which conditions every necessity and every foundation.[13]

The difficulty, according to this system of analysis, is that any fusion of the two radically separated regions of being would bring about a complete annihilation of consciousness:

If what consciousness apprehends as the being toward which it surpasses itself were the pure in-itself, it would coincide with the annihilation of consciousness. But consciousness does not surpass itself toward its annihilation; it does not want to lose itself in the in-itself of identity at the limit of its surpassing. It is for the for-itself as such that the for-itself lays claim to being-in-itself.[14]

But the contradictions or paradox of such a being do not prove, even for Sartre, that it does not exist, but only that it can not be realized as a fusion of the two disparate modes of being into a single Being. Poetic vision moves, however, beyond the form of synthesis which is simply a simultaneous positing of contraries to create an image of being which is absolute transcendence in absolute immanence, the God desired and desiring, consciousness desired and desiring. Ultimately it can be seen that the poetic structures which have been examined in these studies correspond to the structure of that being so closely that far from being opposed to life they are the image of life itself. The suggestions of solipsism and poetic hermeticism which we have seen structually implied in the tendency toward symmetry

[13] *Being and Nothingness,* p. 90.
[14] *Ibid.*

and in the ever-present circle can be understood, in the context of the universalized and 'shared' consciousness which Jiménez achieves in *Animal de fondo*, to correspond to a concept of the being of human reality sufficient in itself, needing no relation to a cause as an 'excuse' for its being nor any consequence as justification for it.

The modern philosophers who have most thoroughly analyzed this being have tended to use anthropomorphic —that is, pathetic—language to refer to its immanent justification, as though only external justification (which entails a problem of infinite regress) could save it from triviality. Thus, Sartre speaks of the 'superfluity' of all being and of the 'absurdity' of human life,[15] and even Heidegger's reference to the 'throwness' of *Dasein* into its 'there' seems to imply a negative judgment resulting from the disappointed expectation of a more deliberately purposeful delivering-over of human existence into its being.[16]

But it is precisely the absence of that kind of pathos in Jiménez which permits him to accept and treat with the seriousness of attitude traditionally called religious the immanent justification of the being of consciousness. The attitude is fundamentally realistic and free from the sentimentality of cynicism, for it retains no

---

[15] Sartre, p. lxvi.

[16] "This characteristic of Dasein's Being—this 'that it is'—is veiled in its "whence" and "whither," yet disclosed in itself all the more unveiledly; we call it the *"thrownness"* of this entity into its "there"; indeed, it is thrown in such a way that, as Being-in-the-world, it is the "there." The expression "thrownness" is meant to suggest the *facticity of its being delivered over.*" (*Being and Time*, p. 174.) Also: "As something thrown, Dasein has been thrown *into existence*. It exists as an entity which has to be as it is and as it can be." (p. 321.)

normative prejudices to suffer disappointment. Doubtless this acceptance is conditioned by a tradition of
religious belief which has made familiar the concept of
a Being who coincides with his own being, one who is
absolute, unconditioned, and sufficient to himself and
at the same time conscious and present to himself. But
the poet's intuition has penetrated all traditional be-
liefs to achieve a direct confrontation with that essence
of human reality which is consciousness and life, of
whose structure and intrinsic worth his art is the reflection.

APPENDIX

Bibliography of first editions of the complete works of poetry of Juan Ramón Jiménez and of the prose works cited in this study:

Almas de violeta. Madrid, 1900.
Ninfeas. Madrid, 1900.
Rimas. Madrid, 1902.
Arias tristes. Madrid, 1903.
Jardines lejanos. Madrid, 1904.
Elegías puras. Madrid, 1908.
Elegías intermedias. Madrid, 1909.
Olvidanzas: Las hojas verdes. Madrid, 1909.
Elegías lamentables. Madrid, 1910.
Baladas de primavera (1907). Madrid, 1910.
La soledad sonora (1908). Madrid, 1911.
Pastorales (1905). Madrid, 1911.
Poemas mágicos y dolientes (1906). Madrid, 1911.
Melancolía (1910–1911). Madrid, 1912.
Laberinto (1910–1911). Madrid, 1913.
Platero y Yo. Madrid, 1914.
Estío (1915). Madrid, 1916.
Platero y Yo (1907–1916). Primera edición completa. Madrid, 1917.
Poesías escojidas (1899–1917). New York, 1917.
Sonetos espirituales (1914–1915). Madrid, 1917.
Eternidades (1916–1917). Madrid, 1918.
Piedra y cielo (1917–1918). Madrid, 1919.
Segunda antolojía poética (1898–1918). Madrid, 1922.
Poesía (1917–1923). Madrid, 1923.
Belleza (1917–1923). Madrid, 1923.
Canción. Madrid, 1936.
La estación total. Buenos Aires, 1946.
Romances de Coral Gables (1939–1942). México, 1948.
Animal de fondo. Con la versión francesa de Lysandro Z. D. Galtier. Buenos Aires, 1949.

Tercera antolojía poética (1908–1953). Madrid, 1957.
Libros de poesía. Ed. Agustín Caballero. Madrid, 1957.
Primeros libros de poesía. Edited by Francisco Garfias. Madrid, 1959.
La corriente infinita (Crítica y evocación). Edited by Francisco Garfias. Madrid, 1961.
El trabajo gustoso (Conferencias). Edited by Francisco Garfias. Mexico, 1961.
La colina de los chopos (Madrid posible e imposible) (1915–1924). Edited by Francisco Garfias. Barcelona, 1963.
Libros inéditos de poesía, 1. Edited by Francisco Garfias. Madrid, 1964.
Dios deseado y deseante. Edited by Antonio Sánchez Barbudo. Madrid, 1964.

INDEX

Designed by Gerard A. Valerio
Composed in Linotype Baskerville by Kingsport Press, Inc.
Printed letterpress by Kingsport Press, Inc. on Warren's 1854
Bound by Kingsport Press, Inc. in GSB Vellum S/622 Maroon